PRAISE FOR LAR'S COACH

I can't express to you how your coaching keeps my career alive!-Shawn

I just wanted to thank you again for the wealth of information you have given me.-Jason

As always, thanks for your support and encouragement and showing me how to think positively and "out of the box!"-Virginia

I had a wonderful time at your class Friday Night and learned so much from you. I was very impressed with you! Thanks for all that you do for me.-Ron

If only there were more helpful people like you!-Jeff

Yay! We did it... I never ever would have gone through with this career if it were not for your encouragement!-Annie

Thank you for all your help and guiding us in the right direction. Tori said she had the best two days in your class than she ever had at that modeling school!. She learned so much. Thank you for making the class available to her.-GiGi

I wanted to write and say thank you, for all of your help with my audition. I got a positive and rapid response from casting!-Chris

I want to thank you so much for all your help this weekend with Michael. What a big difference you have made for him. . . I can see great things to start happening with his career . . . I really enjoyed your knowledge of the acting field and your generosity of that knowledge. You are so kind . . . .
-Colton

We had a great time and I felt truly reinvented with your coaching and methods. WOW! Could not stop talking about you and the experience.-Ed

I really enjoyed the class on Saturday- I'm PUMPED!-Jenna.

I wanted to thank you again... I have never had anyone help me as much as you have in the past week. Your coaching made complete sense to me. I honestly have no clue what I would have done without you! Thank you so much for everything! -Micaela

Shelby LOVED your class last night. I was so impressed with her tape. You did so much more with her in an hour and a half than the three classes at another acting school!.-Penny

I want to thank you for such an informative and useful marketing seminar. You definitely motivated me to kick it up a notch. Again thank you for sharing your knowledge. You are professional, inspirational, and just what the industry needs!!!-Robin

The seminar was very informative and Lar Park Lincoln was great! She was an enthusiastic speaker and gave many useful tips and ideas for all of us to use in the future. -Donna

As I listened to you advising the rest of my classmates, I thought "Lar is soooo in her element!" It is awesome to see people who are using their God-given, natural gifts to help others. You are a natural-born encourager! Thanks for sharing that part of you with the rest of us.-Naima

THANK YOU once again for your infinite wisdom! WOW!-Josh

Get Started, *Not* Scammed

From Finance to Fame

By Lar Park Lincoln

to Matilda—

ImDB.com

Chase that Star!

Lar Park Lincoln

Get Started, *Not* Scammed – From Finance to Fame
Copyright © 2008 by Purely Park Lincoln, Inc.

Cover design by Heather Okun
Interior design by Brad Barton
Cover photography by Mark Roddenberry

ISBN – 978-0-9774505-8-9
LCCN – 2005935895

DEDICATION

To my children, Piper and Trevor - unique, brave, incredible people - for their unwavering support of my creative career; for growing up with a celebrity mom; for dealing with the traveling, the long hours, the feast and the famine; for sharing me with my students and fans; and for giving me the ability to live and coach my motto:

Dream, Believe, Achieve

I love you more than can be expressed in words.
Mom

Table of Contents

© Mary Ann Halpin

Forward

I have been where you are now, wondering how to get started in a new field and badly in need of experience and direction. You have probably found yourself wondering, "Whom can I trust, and which information is believable? Who is using my dreams to benefit himself? Who is not truly invested in my future?" I have been where you are. I have heard all of the exciting stories about being discovered overnight and the scary tales about being scammed by fake talent agents. So how did a five feet four and a half inch army brat go from a mousy little no one to one of nighttime television's *femme fatales*?

Having grown up in the military, I was always the "new kid." I traveled constantly – new schools; new teachers; new assignments. Who would have predicted a simple elementary school classroom assignment would define my destiny and give me a map to my future? My Timeline to Stardom™ began that day, slow and steady, and now I can teach it to you.

We were told to write an essay: "What would we be if we could be anything?" With childhood innocence and adult-like tenacity, I believed if I wrote it down, it would come true. At the time, I did not know about the power of written intention and goal setting. I wrote about three careers, and I even remember the dress I wore when it came time to give what would be the first of many speeches on my way to a career in public speaking.

"I will be an actress, a writer, and a teacher." I looked out over the disbelieving and incredulous eyes of my classroom. I was serious, but to everyone else, it was humorous. Their silence soon erupted into rude laughter. Who would believe an unattractive, thin, "match stick" of a girl with horrible glasses, stringy hair, and a gawky body – not to mention a plain, simple face - could successfully travel the bumpy road to stardom?

I didn't let that stand in my way. I knew I had chosen my career path and I set out to discover how to make it a reality. I won't pretend it was an easy road. Rarely is a successful career. I hit road blocks, setbacks, and brick walls. But just like me, with the proper coaching and education from this book, you can overcome obstacles and make your dreams come true.

In the tenth grade, I had only two pair of shoes and two pair of jeans to make it through the entire school year. I desperately needed a blow-dryer, and a telephone would have helped, too. I had *nothing* with which to start my career. Still, my lack of money wasn't a roadblock; rather, I considered it a slight detour. I knew it was still my destiny, so I stuck to it.

My first agent turned me down eight times. EIGHT! What insanity kept me going back? Despite the rejection, I kept returning, fueled by the tenacity which lives in everyone who ever has had a dream to succeed.

Like many actors before me, modeling was my first chance to break into the industry. Because there was no petite market at the time, I had to really work hard to get bookings, which led me to specialize in several fields, including "parts" modeling.

Because I didn't have a car or driver's license, I spent several years taking two buses across town each way to get to the modeling school where I worked free to gain experience. By working on my own marketing and public relations, opportunities started coming my way--all of this by the time I was fifteen! By taking care of "my business," I started getting booked for jobs more frequently, even over the taller and more attractive models!

Those with the ability to cast liked me because I developed a reputation for staying longer at photo shoots and working longer hours. Everyone came to understand that my work would meet or exceed expectations. School socials and later school *reunions* came and went without me; my career became my business, and it was my top priority! But I must admit that I felt filming a movie was much cooler than attending my ten year reunion. I was living my dream! Finally, a pageant scholarship to a local modeling school gave me the break I needed. During those years, modeling schools had better reputations than they do today and I gratefully credit much of my early success to the education and opportunities it brought me.

> **Lar Says...**
> Not *all* modeling schools are scams, as they are so often portrayed. One of the goals of this book is to help you recognize the difference.

My first Hollywood adventure took place when I was barely seventeen. I wanted to go so badly, yet couldn't afford a plane ticket. I was practicing visualization techniques way before it became popular! I needed a mattress and before my eyes, an opportunity arose. A local mattress store was giving away a free round-trip ticket to Los Angeles with any purchase. I bought the mattress for the free ticket.

Young, eager, and ready to be a star, I made my way to Tinseltown. I had some local training and a fairly amateur actor's portfolio of work and thought I was prepared. I quickly learned that with my southern drawl, no marketable headshots, and no connections, the red carpet did not come rolling out for me.

In less than two weeks, I crawled home wondering what to do. As an old actor's saying goes, "I couldn't get arrested, let alone cast in a movie!" A lesson learned. And so the process of reinventing myself began.

Over the next several years I trained. I took every class I could. I learned the camera, lost the accent, and created my business. Armed with more experience, I returned to Hollywood. I was prepared, experienced, and professional. This time I promised myself *no turning back*!

However, my dream still wasn't realized overnight! It took about a month to get an agent to even meet with me and then I met every agent in LA who would see me. It didn't matter if they were big or small--everyone became an important contact.

I also worked background (extra work) on every project I could find, and I continued to study. Despite my busy acting career and the perpetual odd jobs (even teaching modeling in a charm school), I was also holding down two "day jobs" to make ends meet!

I studied with Tony Barr of the Film Actors Lab and many other wonderful teachers including Margie Haber, who created the Haber Phrase Technique and personally coached me all through my run on *Knots Landing* and many other roles. I highly recommend her studio and her book <u>How to Get the Part ...Without Falling Apart!: Featuring the Haber Phrase Technique for Actors</u>. I credit Sam Christensen for his marketing genius. Kudos also go to Mary Ann Halpin, Los Angeles' premier celebrity photographer with several published works to her credit. The investment I made in her cutting edge headshots was worth every penny. This marked one of the biggest turning points in my career. This team and many others aided in my success. Please don't assume that this was an easy task: it wasn't. I worked hard to get referrals and took every step to insure I would arrive to the job as prepared as possible. My future was up to me. I had to get to auditions, train every day, and get the callback.

I signed with the prestigious William Morris Agency and an incredible management team of Litke Grossbart, who became Litke Grossbart Gayle, who became Litke Grossbart Madden & Gayle, who became – you get the picture! I adored my managers and my agents. Hiring them was one of the best decisions of my career.

After the success of my recurring role on *Knots Landing* and Beverly Hills 90210, my husband of fourteen years died, leaving me alone with two darling babies. I took a much-needed and well-deserved break from full-time acting to be a full-time mother. I continued working on QVC as a celebrity guest host with occasional cameos, guest starring roles and fan appearances.

Coaching seemed a natural choice and I loved it, but I hated the scams that continued to plague our industry and infect my students. Inspiration hit me. I knew I needed to reach a larger audience to protect these families from the heartbreak they were experiencing. After all, I had had a successful career which had been nearly 30 years in the making. Coaching has enabled me to reach thousands of people, helping them start their own careers with open eyes, but a book could help me share my knowledge with even more dreamers and achievers.

Choosing a career in the arts is not an easy road to travel. This business requires persistence, nerves of steel, and faith–in *large* quantities. It takes determination when the odds are against you, and it **is** difficult to get a break. When I started, there were no books to show me the way. I am honored to give you a resource where I can take you by the hand and walk you down the path of creating a successful career.

Consider this book a *work*book. If you had joined the ranks of a large corporation, you would have been handed an Employee Handbook defining guidelines and standards for your new position. This is your Employee Handbook for your acting career. It outlines your daily duties (if you want to succeed). Where a question pops into your head, write it in the margins. When you get a flash of creativity or have one of those ingenious light bulb moments, write these down in this book as quickly as you can! Brainstorming your smallest thoughts and ideas can turn them into action.

I always know when I have an inexperienced new actor in class. Her scripts are neat and clean. Creativity does not work that way! Use the margins – make notes, list dreams, assets, problems, and solutions. List the names of classmates and their emails and phone numbers. Record the names of books and scripts, teachers, casting directors, and anyone or anything else you hear others discussing, and then follow up with a little research. In other words, please make sure this book looks (and is) "acted" upon!

Consider all of your materials, especially books, vital elements in your actor's toolbox. I still cherish one of my first film books by Tony Barr, Acting for the Camera. Most people's books are simply "dog eared." I awoke the morning of one of my on-camera classes to find that my dog, perhaps desiring stardom herself, ingested my class materials.

Upon arrival to Mr. Barr's class, my excuse ("My dog ate my homework") was not well received. Mr. Barr's mouth curled knowingly and quite painfully. His eyebrow arched with the all-knowing look of a seasoned educator. I thought I was about to be asked to leave the program. He surprised me by turning, reaching into a file, and handing me another scene for the evening's lesson.

I keep that dog-chewed book as a reminder that although I couldn't afford another book, I could still afford to press on.

PART I

How Do I Get Started?

Before you **knock 'em** dead in your blockbuster film release, you have to **knock** on a lot of doors!

You must:

1) Know your "type"
2) Get a headshot
3) Create your résumé
4) Find an agent
5) Train
6) Go on auditions
7) Book the job
8) Follow up
9) Repeat steps 1 - 8 for rest of your career

This book will not get you work, but it will give you the core knowledge you need to jump start or re-start a successful acting career. Within each chapter, you will find practical advice and proven examples of what works and what definitely does not!

The modeling and acting business is fun, but it can be hectic and confusing to someone who is not familiar with the industry. However, within the business, it is normal. I call it "Controlled Chaos," because the only consistent thing about a performer's career is the inconsistency. You have to be mentally, emotionally and physically prepared for anything. It will be stressful most of the time, but you will eventually grow accustomed to it. If you have the type of personality that requires regular hours, stable income, and "order," being in front of the camera is probably not the career choice for you. That doesn't mean you can't find rewarding work in the industry. You may be the perfect candidate for a career in producing or another "behind the scenes" type of career. Check out the list of 100 great industry or industry-related jobs in the following article.

100 Cool Things You Can Do In the Biz

There are so many fun, rewarding, and creative places to work both on camera and behind the scenes in the entertainment industry. Each of these is important, and without them, the final product would not be possible. If you are interested in the business – whether in front of or behind the lens - consider one of these fabulous industry jobs below!

Fashion

- Fashion
- Commercial
- Parts modeling
- Plus size
- Print
- Fit models
- Hair models
- Hair shows
- Mannequins
- Car and trade shows
- Makeup and perfume demonstrators

For Actors

- Stage
- Film
- TV
- College student projects
- Union
- Non-union
- Industrials
- Website design
- Spokesperson
- Infomercials
- Live shopping channels
- In-store promotional work
- Convention host/hostess
- Educational programming
- Auctions
- Voiceovers
- Cartoon characters
- TV talk show hosts
- Reporters

Creative Fields

- Advice columnist
- Newspaper columnist
- Editing
- Editing on paper/film
- Graphic artists
- Casting directors
- Director
- Producer
- Writer
- Location scouting
- Merchandising
- Photography
- Makeup artist
- Personal assistants to the stars
- Hairdressers
- Manicurists
- Wardrobe consultants
- Color specialist
- Home and office designs
- Life and career coaching
- Teaching
- Print shop for duplicating
- Agents
- Managers
- Karaoke machine/hostess
- Party and event planner for celebrities
- Charity organizer
- Pageant director/planner
- Office staff for pageants/studios
- Taxi service for families w/kids in the business.
- Assistant or personal assistant to any of the above

Miscellaneous Jobs

- Teamsters
- Dancers
- Singers
- Other specialty performer
- Travel agents that book the "shows"
- Cruise performers
- Modeling school teacher
- Set, prop, and booth design
- Costume designer
- A Vegas style show
- Product promotions at malls and stores
- Script supervisor
- Security personnel, detective
- Bodyguards
- Specialty cosmetic dentistry to the stars
- Plastic surgeon
- Costume jewelry designer
- Lighting director
- Museum tour operator
- Bus tour operator (usually actors in big industry cities)
- Research and updating, assistant to script writers
- Trivia writers
- Motivational Speaker

CHAPTER 1

TYPES OF ACTING AND MODELING

One of the hardest steps on the road to a career in acting and modeling is discovering your particular type, or style. To make the most of your formal training and to truly shine during auditions, you need to know what your style is, who you are, and what kind of role you may be hired to portray.

To do this, you must discover your true self and decide not only the image you wish you to convey but how others already perceive you. Most actors can play many roles, but you can jumpstart your career if you can focus in on a few character "types" while getting started.

Who can you be? That is an important question you should be asking yourself.

Knowing your "type" means identifying *your* specific identity in comparison with industry standards. This helps you determine what roles are available for you. Modeling and acting have different criteria.

> **Lar Says...**
> Please save money at the therapist. Do not confuse your self and your self-esteem with your "type." Learn early to differentiate between reality and acting!

For example, an aspiring model who is under 5'8 inches will not have a career in high fashion runway modeling. She will be better suited for print work, including magazines, newspapers, and catalogues. She would have to be at least 5'8" – 5'10" to be considered seriously for mainstream runway modeling, which reigns predominately in the New York and European markets. A smart working model knows the markets into which she fits, and then she works diligently to create opportunities in those markets.

Areas of Modeling

1) **High Fashion** – Models over 5'8, very thin, runway trained, major metropolitan areas and Europe.

2) **Print** – This is the most common area for models to work. Must have extensive photo portfolios. These models are used for advertising campaigns in magazines, catalogues, newspapers, billboards, and other types of print. One burgeoning area of print modeling is "microstock photography." This is where you are hired and photographed in a series of looks. These stock photos are then sold to various companies, but because they are sold after the shoot (rather than before), you may see yourself on a product label and never even realize you did the job!

3) **Parts** – Parts modeling is a very specific field that require excellent hands or feet or other body parts. Being less than 5'6", I was a very successful parts model. My tiny feet, small ears, blue eyes and "cute" belly button afforded me many years of supplemental income.

4) **Plus size** – These are models who wear size twelve and above. Thankfully, this market has become more popular and now you see these models more frequently.

5) **Spokesmodel** – This model is the "face" of a company. She represents the company at conventions, trade shows, and shopping channels.

6) **Product** – Professional models that appear natural or like "real people." They appear in department or grocery stores "live" promoting various products.

7) **Commercial** – Models who portray "real" people (as opposed to glamorous) in commercials and advertisements.

Areas of Acting

1) **Theatre/Stage** – Actors who perform onstage; for example, Broadway, regional theatre, and dinner theatre.

2) **Television** – Actors on television, series, mini-series, and reality shows.

3) **Film** – Actors in feature, shorts, independent, and competition films.

4) **Commercial** – Actors in television commercials, Podcasts, computer ads, web commercials and so on.

5) **Voice Over** – Actors who voice characters in animated films, cartoons, video games, radio, commercials, and in marketing materials.

6) **Spokesactor**: Similar to a spokesmodel, spokesactors are the faces of companies and products for shopping channels, commercials, and tradeshows.

7) **Industrial:** Actors who portray "real people" in company training or educational productions.

8) **Background/Extras/Atmosphere:** Actors are used to create believability in the scene in television or film. They are true stars – just no one knows it! Imagine how dull a show would be if the audience never saw any environment or background actors around the "star."

9) **Television, award shows, and talk show audiences:** A day job for actors who fill-in seats to help create the appearance of a full audience for taping.

10) **Stand In:** Producers match the height, weight, and coloring of key actors on weekly series and feature films. They are needed for lighting each scene to avoid exhausting the principal players. This is a very important job! Lighting is critical and these workers help the entire production.

11) **Specialty Performers:** Actors who can dance and sing or have other unique skills like mime or magic. They often appear in specialty shows, cruise ships, amusement parks, and casino shows.

Where you live is an important key to the type of work available at a given time. If you are living on the West Coast, you may want to concentrate on film, television, and commercial work. Living on the East Coast, you have more opportunities in areas such as theater or high fashion modeling. Throughout the Midwest, the most common work will be industrials, print, commercial, and back ground work. Keep in mind student films, independent films, and television often shoot on location. You may have an opportunity to audition for these as well.

Decide on a primary focus in acting or modeling which *makes sense* for where you currently live. Despite the location, you must closely examine your field, study your craft, and keep working toward a specific goal. Consistent training and proper marketing should eventually get you where you want to be. Even celebrity actors and actresses keep training. I still have a personal coach in both New York and Los Angeles. Only a new actor that has booked a couple of jobs who now think they "know it all" and fools believe they no longer need coaching!

> **Lar Says...**
> Start where you are. This is a common theme reiterated in both life coaching and in acting classes. Another way to think about it is this: begin where you can. Know what your strengths are.

Being able to adapt to the work in your region is also very important. Growing up in the military, I traveled often and quickly learned to adjust to my surroundings. When I lived in Dallas, I modeled; in Colorado, I auditioned for film; and in Europe, I was contracted for an extensive modeling tour. When I made the permanent move to Los Angeles, I focused on my true dream of television and film work.

The point is this: adaptability is vital. Whatever the job brings your way – bad weather, awkward hours, and uncomfortable accommodations – don't let anything take your mind off the work. I once shot a film in Yugoslavia in below zero temperatures. The director, Bruce Block, found a simple way to help his actors keep focus: He'd provide M&Ms, a luxurious treat we didn't have while we worked so far from home, and encouragement by saying, "Just one more take."

Character "Types"

Most actors can and want to play many types of roles. However, if you focus on three to six specific character types, you narrow down the huge odds that are against you. This is not meant to typecast you in the "old fashioned" sense of the word but to put you in the most likely areas where you can get paying work. The types listed below are only suggestions but cover most of the roles which appear in some variation in television and film. Types do not apply as strictly in stage work.

Take a look at the following worksheet on character types. Can you find several roles you would be able to play?

Now take a moment to complete one of the four surveys. Circle any type of character you feel you could play. Use the remaining three surveys, or feel free to copy more, and have your friends and family give you their opinions. You may be surprised to see patterns emerge as those who know you best circle the same types. Remember, this is not a reflection of just your personality but an exercise in narrowing down the roles you seem most likely to portray.

How does this exercise help you? By defining specific character types in which you are most likely to be cast, you have begun to create your marketing plan. Later in this book, you'll learn more about this, including photo sessions. Knowing your type allows you to better target your submissions, thus raising your chances of being called in for an audition.

Robert

Cristie

Zander

Character "Type" Worksheet

Actor's Name: _____ Date: _____

Worksheet Completed By: _____

Accountant	Fast Food Worker	Nice Girl/Guy
Alcoholic	Funny	Nurse
Artist	Gang Member	Player
Banker	Girl Next Door	Politician
Bitch	Glamour Queen	Postman
Blue Collar Worker	Greedy Stock Broker	Professor
Bookworm	Hair Dresser	Prostitute
Bossy Kid	Hero	School Teacher
Boy Next Door	Hippie	Scientist
Brat	Ingénue	Secretary
Cafeteria Worker	Intellectual	Serious
Chatty Neighbor	Jock or Cheerleader	Sexy Guy/Girl
Church Lady	Know-It-All	Soccer Mom
Convict	Lawyer	The Best Friend
Dad	Leading Lady	The Jealous One
Delivery Person	Leading Man	Vamp
Doctor	Mentally Disturbed	Victim
Drug Addict	Mom	Villain
Drug Dealer	Murderer	Waiter
Executive	Nerd	White Collar Worker

Character "Type" Worksheet

Actor's Name: _____ Date: _____

Worksheet Completed By: _____

Accountant	Fast Food Worker	Nice Girl/Guy
Alcoholic	Funny	Nurse
Artist	Gang Member	Player
Banker	Girl Next Door	Politician
Bitch	Glamour Queen	Postman
Blue Collar Worker	Greedy Stock Broker	Professor
Bookworm	Hair Dresser	Prostitute
Bossy Kid	Hero	School Teacher
Boy Next Door	Hippie	Scientist
Brat	Ingénue	Secretary
Cafeteria Worker	Intellectual	Serious
Chatty Neighbor	Jock or Cheerleader	Sexy Guy/Girl
Church Lady	Know-It-All	Soccer Mom
Convict	Lawyer	The Best Friend
Dad	Leading Lady	The Jealous One
Delivery Person	Leading Man	Vamp
Doctor	Mentally Disturbed	Victim
Drug Addict	Mom	Villain
Drug Dealer	Murderer	Waiter
Executive	Nerd	White Collar Worker

Character "Type" Worksheet

Actor's Name: _____ Date: _____

Worksheet Completed By: _____

Accountant	Fast Food Worker	Nice Girl/Guy
Alcoholic	Funny	Nurse
Artist	Gang Member	Player
Banker	Girl Next Door	Politician
Bitch	Glamour Queen	Postman
Blue Collar Worker	Greedy Stock Broker	Professor
Bookworm	Hair Dresser	Prostitute
Bossy Kid	Hero	School Teacher
Boy Next Door	Hippie	Scientist
Brat	Ingénue	Secretary
Cafeteria Worker	Intellectual	Serious
Chatty Neighbor	Jock or Cheerleader	Sexy Guy/Girl
Church Lady	Know-It-All	Soccer Mom
Convict	Lawyer	The Best Friend
Dad	Leading Lady	The Jealous One
Delivery Person	Leading Man	Vamp
Doctor	Mentally Disturbed	Victim
Drug Addict	Mom	Villain
Drug Dealer	Murderer	Waiter
Executive	Nerd	White Collar Worker

Character "Type" Worksheet

Actor's Name: _____ Date: _____

Worksheet Completed By: _____

Accountant	Fast Food Worker	Nice Girl/Guy
Alcoholic	Funny	Nurse
Artist	Gang Member	Player
Banker	Girl Next Door	Politician
Bitch	Glamour Queen	Postman
Blue Collar Worker	Greedy Stock Broker	Professor
Bookworm	Hair Dresser	Prostitute
Bossy Kid	Hero	School Teacher
Boy Next Door	Hippie	Scientist
Brat	Ingénue	Secretary
Cafeteria Worker	Intellectual	Serious
Chatty Neighbor	Jock or Cheerleader	Sexy Guy/Girl
Church Lady	Know-It-All	Soccer Mom
Convict	Lawyer	The Best Friend
Dad	Leading Lady	The Jealous One
Delivery Person	Leading Man	Vamp
Doctor	Mentally Disturbed	Victim
Drug Addict	Mom	Villain
Drug Dealer	Murderer	Waiter
Executive	Nerd	White Collar Worker

Defining Your Image

Now list your 6 most commonly selected types.

1. _____

2. _____

3. _____

4. _____

5. _____

6. _____

Make notes and research any stars you feel are similar to your character types.

Then, using the information you have gathered, create and design your own unique combination of styles for photo sessions and marketing materials.

An Expert Says...

Developing an Identity

Sam Christensen
www.SamChristensen.com

Developing an identity, according to Mr. Christensen, gives you a memorable factor others don't have. Knowing how you are perceived is vital to how casting directors and directors perceive you. If your photos and your packaging do not reflect the reality of who you are, you are wasting valuable time, money and worse yet, not getting cast.

Knowing your "types" and embracing them is the cornerstone of longevity in your acting career. Sam is considered the best in the image business and believes that product identity is essential to all marketing. In this case, you are your product.

The ability of the director, producer, casting director and even the audience to remember a particular actor is the challenge facing you and all actors who are not yet 'names.' What does your image say about you? Is it saying what you want it to say?

He tells those who come to him for advice to ask themselves how are they singled out among the throngs of actors submitted for the roles? Are you regularly on lists of actors who will be seen for significant roles? Are your special, unique qualities recognized and are they translating into opportunities?

Mr. Christensen says, if you don't give photographers themes for the shoot, or "types," you just end up with nice pictures, not pictures that show the real you. He suggests that actors view themselves as their own studio and create an image based on the reality of how they are perceived and how they view themselves.

An Expert Says...

Self-Management for Actors

Bonnie Gillespie, Author
www.CricketFeet.com

Having a professional attitude will really put you above your competition. As they say, "You are always auditioning for your *next* audition."

Your submission envelope nominates you. Your headshot seconds the nomination. Your cover letter is your campaign speech. Your résumé' votes you into office. Your audition is your term. Callbacks are how you're doing in the polls. Booking the job is your re-election. Once you're an incumbent, it's easier to stay in office. A string of jobs is your career.

As an actor your *job* is auditions and auditioning. Every time you have an audition, you are putting in a day of work.

In regard to marketing, make sure you sign off every post on internet forums, every email you send, and every cover letter you write with a link to your URL in order to get traffic headed to your site.

CHAPTER 2

PAGEANTRY

It is straight out of a little girl's fantasy: A sparkling crown is placed upon her perfectly coiffed hair, gleaming in the spotlight. The months of preparation, the excitement, the gowns, and the etiquette all come together to create a perfect ending.

Many girls participate in a pageant for the experience, but some turn the competitions into a scholastic opportunity, cashing in on phenomenal scholarships. Those that win the coveted title have something to be cherished for the rest of their lives.

While some people confuse pageants with performing and modeling, it actually involves an entirely different set of standards. Modeling, acting, and pageantry are separate fields. Even winning an acting or modeling competition at a pageant is not equivalent to mainstream industry standards. These very specific requirements vary with each pageant system.

The death of JonBenét Ramsey in 1996 brought little girl pageants into the public limelight. At that point, many systems had evolved to the point where six year old girls were made up with big hair, removable false teeth, and grotesquely mature make-up.

Perhaps as a result of public outcry over photos of JonBenét Ramsey that surfaced after her death, pageants have experienced a change. Several pageants today prefer no makeup on children, and young ladies are expected to look their ages. The more natural pageants celebrate scholastic achievements, volunteer work, and avoid swimsuit and other body-baring competitions.

The new trend in scholastic and personality-based pageants is gaining public support. Personally, I don't think it is wise for girls under the age of 8 to compete in any type of pageant. They lack the maturity and self-esteem to understand that not winning doesn't mean they aren't winners. My own daughter won the title of Miss Texas Junior Teen 2006-2007 after 6 years of competing, and it has been a great experience for the whole family. We have traveled to exciting new places, and she has inspired many other girls to try to achieve their dreams.

Pageant requirements

While every pageant system is different, most pageants will have a similar basic set of rules. Carefully read your system's individual requirements before competing.

You can expect to compete in some sort of interview, either business or current event-based. Furthermore, there will probably be an evening gown presentation and some sort of runway or casual wear competition. Most pageants incorporate a dance number (or several) in the finale, and you may need to purchase either an entire performance outfit or wear jeans and a coordinating pageant T-shirt and sneakers.

What are some associated costs to be expected?

The cost of participating in a pageant can be anywhere from very extreme to quite manageable. It all depends on how you budget your money.

Gowns are a large portion of scoring, and they can be very expensive. However, a savvy shopper can find a $2500 gown for $300. You may need to hire a tailor to achieve a perfect fit. Wedding gowns are also an option, and these can be purchased very affordably during the wedding "off season." You can recycle the gowns from one pageant to the next, or take turns between two favorites. Wear comfortable shoes, like those worn by dancers, under your gown.

Other fees may include:

- Entrance fees ranging from $50 to $250
- Outfits required for special numbers
- Hotel and other travel expenses
- Hair cut, style, and color
- Facial costs (including waxing) if needed
- Photography
- Tickets for the main event ranging from $10 to $20 each

What happens during a pageant week or weekend?

- Rehearsals for dance numbers
- Fittings
- Practicing for interviews and introductions
- Waiting patiently for your turn
- The final event

Many families and friends that have come to support you don't realize that most judging has taken place during competitions preceding the event. At the actual pageant night performance, they will see a group that has been narrowed to a manageable number of contestants.

What is the ultimate goal of pageants?

A crown, while quite beautiful, does not hold a great deal of value. Most girls compete to learn self esteem. On top of that, the feeling of accomplishment is immeasurable. What a girl does with her title is entirely up to her, but it does provide an excellent stepping stone to greatness. My daughter chose to work with a local children's hospital and to become a mediator at her school.

After winning, distribute a press release to all local papers in your area. You will want to include a photo and enhance the release with a short personal story. As a title holder, it will be important to associate yourself with a charity so that your new title can benefit others, too. As a volunteer for that charity, you can sign autographs or pose for pictures, attend ribbon cuttings, and volunteer at public events. While a title can be a stepping stone and résumé builder, that cannot be its only function. The girl under the crown must make her year's reign important and seek ways to enhance both her community and herself.

> **Lar Says...**
> I highly advise keeping a cooler of snacks and drinks on hand as well as plenty of hair spray, cell phones charged, and a sense of humor! Even though it may not be their thing, bring the males in the family. All brothers, fathers, and grandfathers are recruited to escort the beauties across the stage in formal wear. They are the most nervous, and this allows for priceless family pictures and memories.

Piper Lincoln
2006-2007 National American Miss Junior Teen Texas

I became the *2006-2007 National American Miss Jr. Teen Texas,* and I am extremely excited about my new title! Being crowned was exciting, thrilling and proved to me the value of effort, persistence and preparation!! And it was a really fun way to celebrate turning 16!! I graciously accepted the crown and the responsibility of being a role model for others! I won a college scholarship and many fun prizes!

I began competing with the National American Miss Pageant program when I was 11 years old. *This pageant is unlike any other*. There is no swimsuit competition, no makeup allowed on girls under 13 and only age appropriate makeup for the older girls. National American Miss promotes the building of self-esteem and confidence. I compete in this pageant for those reasons and I strongly support what the people at National American Miss have created: a scholarship program designed to empower young women with business and presentation skills. This is a pageant where physical beauty is not the determining factor.

After competing with this pageant for 5 years, I have gained so much more confidence than I ever thought possible!

I can certainly say that being in a pageant takes tons of work and I have definitely worked my hardest to get this far in the pageant world! I was fourth runner-up after only my second pageant, and from there second runner-up. *Last year I took first runner up and won both Miss Personality and the Runway modeling competition.*

My advice to all young women who have a goal: Keep trying until *you* are satisfied with the results! Keep practicing and working at your goals, and you will get far! Keep a smile on your face, and don't get too stressed out! Just show who you really are, because that's the girl that can make a difference.

Matilda,
Good luck
in all you do!
Piper

Q&A With Micaela Johnson
Miss Nebraska USA

"Go confidently in the direction of your dreams. Live the life you've always imagined."

Why did you enter the pageant and what do you hope to gain from the experience?

Initially, I entered this pageant to work towards a goal of developing strong communication skills. However, throughout my pageant preparation I've come to realize that it's much more then an opportunity, it's a job and one that I'm ready for! I hope that through this experience I will develop a better understanding for who I am and be able to apply my leadership skills within my community.

What social causes mean the most to you?
There are many social causes that are important to me, but the one issue that I would spend my year focusing on is Childhood Obesity. I feel that this is a serious issue facing many children today and the key is being able to educate parents and children on ways to lead a healthy lifestyle.

What is one thing you have learned in life and who did you learn it from?
My Dad taught me one of the most important lessons in my life. He taught me to never let anything or anyone stand in the way of achieving my dreams.

What are a few of your favorite hobbies?
Some of my hobbies include scrapbooking, sewing, designing websites, rhinestoning EVERYTHING, shopping, fitness classes, and cooking the best Dr. Pepper Cake!!! Yum!

What personal achievement are you most proud of?
The personal achievement which I am most proud of is being a Dallas Cowboys Cheerleader. It was an opportunity of a lifetime, allowing me to experience things that I had never dreamt possible.

An Expert Says...

Developing Confidence

Steven Mays, Director,
National American Miss
www.namiss.com

My background was not in pageantry. I am an oil man and I was asked to judge a pageant because I was an interviewer and recruiter for the Chevron corporation. Coaching students at the University of Texas on how to excel at job interviews coincided with Chevron interviewing graduates! So I learned both sides.

Honestly, I wasn't that interested in judging my first pageant, but I was sold when I saw that more than half of the contestants could out-interview the MBAs I was interviewing! That made a big impression on me!!

I've had the pleasure of working with over 40,000 contestants during the quarter decade I have been producing shows and have learned people have many different opinions about pageants, and many are stereotypes. However, not all pageantry is the same. Each pageant has its own unique style, so it's important you research and find the one that is right for you.

Twenty years ago I did a survey to learn what families wanted from pageantry. After speaking to over 200 families I found out the one common goal that they wanted for their child was confidence. Interestingly the kids wanted confidence too! New friends, and a fun family vacation also, but one thing that really stood out was the *lack of interest in makeup!*

At the National American Miss Pageants, no makeup is allowed on young girls. We are not focusing on a false type of beauty, a made up kind of persona for the evening. We feel each girl is uniquely created and God doesn't make mistakes, so they are great just like they are. We also don't believe we need a swimsuit competition. The contestants wear matching outfits for their on stage routines, and it works great! The contestants feel comfortable and so does the audience.

At National American Miss the majority of scoring is on communication, whether it's the on stage personal introduction, the personal interviews with each judge, or the escorted formal wear. Communication is the key unique difference about National American Miss.

I always tell people to check things out. When you go shopping you evaluate, you look for options, you get recommendations. I say the same thing whether it's pageants, a talent agency, an acting coach, or a dance company – check their references. Check with the Better Business Bureau to see if they are a member. Keep in mind that you have choices like everything else. You are the shopper. You are the buyer. You have choices. Ask questions so you can make an informed decision.

Sina

CHAPTER 3

THE WINNING HEADSHOT

If you can learn how to shoot and edit your best headshots, you will save thousands of dollars! If not, you will probably waste thousands.

One of the most costly mistakes made by beginner and experienced actors alike is not learning how to shoot or select a great headshot. By relying on others to tell you what to wear and what your shots should look like, you will waste countless dollars and time taking pictures that will not work for you. One of the best ways to learn is to study what works for successful actors -- and what does not.

On the following pages, you will see before and after shots as well as my professional evaluations to help you learn how to shoot a picture for your most important calling card.

There are two industry rules concerning this tool:

- Rule # 1 – You *must* have a great headshot.
- Rule # 2 – See Rule # 1.

You cannot begin this career without a marketable headshot. This is your first step to getting started and the single most important business decision you will make. This is also an expense which you are going to regularly incur as you continue to work. I instruct all of my clients to shoot new pictures every six months and encourage you to do the same.

Your headshot should make you shine, stand out, and get the call for auditions. You do not have to be the most handsome actor, the most beautiful woman, or the tallest model to have a great photo. This tool is used for two reasons:

1. To help you find an agent to represent you and,
2. To submit for auditions both by mailing a hard copy and emailing an electronic version sized 640x480 pixels or smaller.

When you start, you will only need one or two headshots to interest an agent. Eventually, you will need to create a portfolio of various looks for different characters. Shooting that first great picture can be an adventure.

Lar Says...

For actors, your headshot needs to display who you *really* are, not who you want to be. A smart actor will have different headshots for various characters they can portray. Each of mine are designed to create a specific look to help my agent "sell me" as a well-rounded actor. I used one to get me roles like the conniving Linda Fairgate I played on *Knots Landing*. My other headshots helped me land roles such as a desperate teenage prostitute and an undercover narcotics agent.

With planning, it can be easy and fun to create a "look" for yourself that can help you stand apart from the crowd. For starters, photo sessions are more affordable than in the past, and the process of digitalization has taken away many of the costs such as film, proof sheets, and valuable waiting time. Retouching is now simple. It used to have to be done directly on a print, by hand. No longer must sessions be rescheduled due to last minute breakouts, sleepless nights, scrapes, bruises, and so on. The purpose of retouching is to clean up imperfections in the shot. They may have been technical such as dust on the camera lens, distracting backgrounds or shadows. Retouching may also be used to remove blemishes, soften lines and correct make-up mistakes.

I once coached an actor who had developed a terrible allergy on his eyelid – a horrible rash that was inflamed and red. The worst part was that he had booked with a photographer who had flown in from out of town. If the actor had rescheduled, it might have taken months to get a new date. On top of that, he was also responsible for the expense of the photographer's travel (which no one wants to pay *twice*!). But with digital retouching, this was not a problem. A few keystrokes later, he looked like his normal unblemished self.

In another case, I coached a thirteen-year-old girl who had missing teeth on one side of her smile. They had grown in partially, but it was a noticeable distraction. This is a very common problem for teens but not for our shoot day. The digital expert was able to "grow" her teeth into place for a subtle change that gave her a beautiful smile that was *not fake*. As a matter of fact, it was to be her smile very soon. Her teeth just needed a very short amount of time to catch up to her headshot.

Maddie

Retouching can also be done to brighten smiles that are in the process of being whitened. Because photographers now have the ability to correct photographs easily, shoots don't have to be rescheduled, talent doesn't have to wait forever before getting their shots, and no one needs to be angry with Mother Nature for acne outbreaks on the day of a shoot.

However, it is very important that you realize that these techniques are to be used to simply "clean up" a photograph, not to create a face that isn't there.

> **WARNING:**
> Do not redesign your nose, erase your wrinkles, or drastically change your face. Casting directors want to see you, albeit the best you, *not* a fake retouched version.

Most people seeking my coaching services also ask for advice on promoting themselves. Many will send in their school picture, wedding picture, or vacation pictures. Is this acceptable when requesting representation from an agent? No, and it's not an impression you want to make. It is fine, however, for coaching if you are requesting advice. This industry has very specific requirements, and if you want to compete with those who are successful, you have to understand the requirements.

Without fail, I see the same mistakes repeatedly when it comes to headshots. Here is a list of common errors.

- Excessive jewelry, such as a ring on every finger
- Too much makeup
- Hair too flat or too over-styled, "big" hair
- Poor hygiene
- Inappropriate wardrobe
- Hands on the face
- Squinted eyes
- Dead stare or "shark eyes"
- Fake or forced smiles
- Expressions with scowls or frowns
- Suggestive or inappropriate poses
- Poor lighting
- Shots that are out of focus
- Photographs taken on a home computer web cam
- Family pictures with the family cropped out
- Prop usage in the shot such as cigarettes or hats
- Busy backgrounds which distract from the actor
- Passive, uninvolved body language
- Tilted heads or chins turned away from the camera

Here are many of the most common horrible, rotten, lousy headshots.

The excessive jewelry and poor hand placement make this beautiful actress appear unapproachable.

The titled head and passive expression gives an "I don't care" impression – and if you don't care, neither will a prospective agent.

Busy pattern, heavy jewelry, unkempt hair, and passive expression are not attractive.

Heavily patterned wardrobe, distracting jewelry, unstyled hair, and blank expression all combine to make this shot unflattering.

Turtlenecks tend to compress the face, add weight, and hide the neck. With pursed lips and lifeless hair, this is not an effective headshot.

A common mistake is to try to make the background "interesting." A headshot is about you, but this one is all about the ivy. Her hair disappears into the background.

Always take into consideration your face shape. With a round face, avoid round collars, jewelry, and big, round curls.

Poor posture, a frightened expression, and dull wardrobe and jewelry create a disengaged feeling to this headshot.

Hats are generally a poor choice for headshots as they hide the face and put the eyes in deep shadow.

A Special Thank You to these professional actors for allowing me to demonstrate poor headshots in order to give you visual teaching examples.

Heather

Michelle

Catherine

Examples of the most common horrible, rotten, lousy poses.

A Special Thank You to this professional actor for allowing me to demonstrate poor posing in order to give you visual teaching examples.

Alexis

- Do not separate fingers on the hands, creating a claw.
- Angles and curves are better than stiff and straight.
- Avoid showing underarms.

Remember, there are many different types of photography. Those who shoot weddings and who create beautiful graduation portraits may not know the standards for shooting actor headshots. Do not use "glamour studios" either. Research "headshot photographer" in your area and ask to see examples before you commit to hiring anyone.

What steps can *you* personally take to achieve an awesome shot? Study the headshots on the following pages. Let them be your guide.

Do you see a sparkle in the actors' eyes? A pleasant expression? Can you immediately identify what types of characters the actor in the photo can play? Does the headshot easily identify the actor's strength? In other words, if you were a casting director, what character would you cast this person as?

As you develop a trained eye, you will begin to edit the best pictures immediately. If you have to labor over a selection of shots, I can guarantee they are not good enough. You only need one or two great images per photo session. Eliminate the shots which have an obvious flaw. The few left are the only ones which count. Give the leftovers to family and friends if you cannot bear to part with them.

Some of the headshots included in the examples would be considered "winners" at auditions. There are some that would not be considered appropriate for various reasons. Can you tell the difference? Focus on the poses, hairstyles, wardrobe, and facial expressions.

Technically and professionally speaking, you should not take your own pictures or use mall portrait studio pictures or school photos for agent submissions – UNLESS it is your only option AND you are in a very small market with a limited number of agents. If you do choose to use non-industry professional photos, the suggestions below will be very helpful. Furthermore, if you are a seasoned pro but your materials are not working for you, the tips will still apply.

- Use a clean, simple, non-busy background that does not distract from your face. Solid colors, blue, gray, green, and pastels. Leave black and white backgrounds to professionals as they are more difficult to light.
- Do not use makeup on children.
- Try to capture your personality in the photos.

- Make sure the eyes are wide open and relaxed.
- Keep clothes simple and not distracting.
- Shoot on the same level with your subject.
- Keep headshots "straight on" as opposed to leaning heads or a "cheerleader" pose. As far as headshots go, a fully tilted or angled head looks very unprofessional.

Designing Your Photo Shoot

It is vitally important that you learn how to design your own marketing campaign. If you do not, you will join the club with the many other utterly confused talents wondering why your headshots are not working for you.

When you hire a photographer and a set coach, you are paying for their experience, trained eye and up-to-date industry knowledge. Find a coach who is willing to help you before you book a photo session. Before digital photography, you would make an appointment and physically meet the photographer to look at their portfolio. Today, photographers have their portfolios on-line so you can view their work at your convenience. The interview can be done on the phone or by email. The work you see on a photographer's website is the work that you will get. If you do not like the "style" you see, choose a different photographer.

A photo session can easily cost you anywhere from $300 to $800 for two to three different looks. Before committing to any price, make sure you read and discuss your agreement with the photographer carefully. The price quoted should include the photographer's release so that you can duplicate your photo at any time. Also included should be an agreement of when and how you can re-shoot your session with the current photographer if none of your pictures are usable.

After you hire a photographer, you will need to design your photo shoot. Everyone needs a clean, basic, and straight forward pose with just your natural everyday look. For example, if you are a teenage boy, you may want a headshot with a jean

> **Lar Says...**
> Consider hiring a coach to attend the session with you or to help you prepare ahead of time. My photo shoot service, On Set Coaching, is designed to help actors get the most from their experience. After personally consulting with an actor, we determine three basic looks that will help the individual on his or her career path. By designing these looks, we can create a photo shoot which will portray the actor in several ways. This will then give the agent different options from which to choose when submitting pictures for auditions.

jacket and a t-shirt. If you can pull off a "bad boy" look, you may also want to wear a dark jacket to create a "rougher" feel.

In order to prevent disappointment later, work in cooperation with your photographer. Digital photography allows you to see the pictures immediately and decide if the session is going in the right direction. After looking at a digital proof with the photographer, *this is the time to make decisions about whether you need to make hair, make-up, or wardrobe changes* (the main reasons sessions fail). Headshots today are shot in color, and reproduction costs are the same now for either color or black and white. Lithographs (also called Lithos), when produced in a good lab, are equal to or even better looking than photo reprint, and they are much less expensive.

Wardrobe

Not every aspect of a quality photograph takes place behind the camera lens. Partnering with your photographer helps create winning headshots.

Your responsibility in this partnership includes choosing the right wardrobe for your photo session. The clothes you wear should complement your body type and not overpower you. You should prepare several different "looks" which define a **type** (see your list from Chapter 1) that closely resembles the characters for which you would be cast. This is not to be confused with costuming. *Suggest* the character type, do not **dress** the character.

When it comes to your wardrobe, it is as important as your face, skin and hair. Remember to bring several items to the photo shoot from which to choose. Here are some general headshot wardrobe guidelines:

Do	Do Not
Wear jacket and shirt which are matte and solid in color.	Wear loud and flashy outfits that may be distracting.
Wear clothes which are opaque and flatter your skin and eye color.	Wear clothes that reflect light or are made with shiny material.

Do	Do Not
Consider jeans and a jean jacket an option, as they are a good choice.	Wear t-shirts or clothing with logos, slogans, or pictures.
Use jewelry sparingly (such as a simple string of pearls).	Wear reflective, flashy, large, excessive, or dangling jewelry.
Layer your tops for a different look.	Wear turtlenecks.
Consider an open, complementary neckline.	Wear overly plunging tops if you are a woman.
Remove the lenses from your glasses if they reflect the light.	Wear round necklines if you have a round face.
Feature the neckline, not the hemline.	Wear V-necks if you have a pointed chin.
Wear clean, pressed outfits.	Wear wrinkled, dirty clothing.
Use patterns sparingly.	Allow patterns to detract from the subject of the photo: You!

Immediately we notice the watch distracts from the actor's face. In general, hands should be kept out of headshots. The pale wardrobe, pale skin, and light hair wash out the entire headshot.

In this handsome "after" shot, the actor comes to life. The use of more complementary tones in the wardrobe and background along with a bright, relaxed smile make for the winning headshot!

Maury

Do You Have "It"?

I have spent years studying actors' tapes, headshots and résumés. It is very common for actors, models and parents to solicit my advice about their current photo. They want to know if they have "It." I always tell them, "Talent is subjective and technique is not, and no one can guarantee whether you have "It" from one headshot."

So what is "It?" The answer is complicated. The "It" factor is that rare combination of talent, looks, style, determination, and creativity that comes wrapped in one package. This "It" factor makes an agent want to represent you and the public idolize you. When you have "It," everyone knows. You do not have to have "It" to have a successful career; however, most well-known stars do have "It."

Remember, winning photos are not an exact science. Different agents have different philosophies and work with different goals in mind. Naturally, models and actors use different types of headshots. Models will use stylistic shots to show their fashion potential and actors will use realistic poses. Still, the basic requirements are the same.

For actors, photos need to be clear, sharp, and in focus. They should stand out from the thousands of others in the crowd. The actor's eyes must shine and sparkle. This technique is often achieved by the photographer's assistant using a gold or silver card or a reflector held under the face to bounce light back into the eyes.

As you study different headshots, you will notice the distinction this effect can have. If the eyes are dead and dull they look like "shark eyes." Unless casting for "Nemo" or "Jaws," no casting director will invite that look for an audition.

Headshots are special, so think of your session as being a special day. If you were preparing for any other special event, you would lay out your clothes and accessories in advance. You would pay extra attention to your appearance. You are investing a great deal of money in your shots. Invest an equal amount of preparation. Your diligence and enthusiasm will be rewarded. You'll brim with confidence in the audition room as you pass out the eye-catching, brilliantly arranged shots.

An actor brought me a headshot in which his lips were chapped and peeling. He had submitted this photo to producers and industry professionals, and was wondering why he wasn't booking work. Quite simply, his look did not define him as a character. If he were intentionally going for a rough look, we would have designed the wardrobe and his facial expressions to reflect that. In this case, the actor had never been taught how to design a headshot photo session. He did not know how plan the process.

When it comes to your headshot investment, be sure your appearance is the best it can be.

Different Look, Same Day

You will want different looks for different headshots. In order to create more than one look at a single photo session, try the following tips:
- Changing outfits – as simple as layering T-shirts, tanks, jacket
- Changing makeup – adding stronger eyes, lips, blusher, bronzer
- Changing hair – curling, straightening
- Changing jewelry – from casual to dressy
- Start with a simple, clean straightforward pose
- Add a more "designed" character actor look.
- A T-shirt in white or black with a jean jacket
- A leather jacket or preppy jacket

Change by:
- Switch to a drop earring from a stud.
- Pin hair up or add a hairpiece.
- Pull hair into a ponytail, use a barrette to pull the sides back, curl or wave your hair with a curling iron.

Allow ample time to prepare. For instance, it is common for men to have a photo shoot with a full beard, scruffy look, and rugged clothing. They can quickly clean up and change clothes for an entirely different "look."

For the women it would be a similar process. Start with less makeup and then add if you need more. Your first shot might be as casual as a shirt and jacket, minimal makeup, and simple hairstyle. Your second look can be dressier with more intense makeup, false or curled eyelashes, and lined lips as opposed to just a gloss for shine.

To achieve different looks on the same day, start by laying out several choices and deciding what your goals are for the shoot. Review these beforehand with your photographer and coach, so everyone understands your unique and individual needs. Involve your team in your plans, and the outcome will reflect a collaborative work instead of a disjointed one.

Lar

You may have noticed that the teen on the front cover of this book looks very similar to the author on the back cover. Both are yours truly, shot on the same day. Changes in hair, wardrobe, makeup, and expression created both a young and a sophisticated Lar.

James

Brooke

It is *not* the photographer's job to teach you how to pose. Experienced photographers are very capable offering advice to better enhance your look. However, that is the exception to the rule. Do not try to make your photographer your stylist.

Bring a few photos of styles and looks you feel are right for you. For instance, you could bring the photo of an actress or model whose hairstyle you would like your stylist to duplicate. Remember most stars have stylists designing their looks. Do not reinvent the wheel – study current magazine and television shows for up-to-date looks.

Several of these "before" shots are new actors who had not been trained or coached for a professional shot. With a little training, they are transformed into marketable actors with star potential.

Creating three different looks is a great way for new actors with a limited budget to get more photos in the same shoot. The benefits to this "three in one" session will far outweigh the additional planning and costs that would have taken place in a normal setting.

The goal is to wear attire with hair and makeup as close to the photo as possible when attending auditions. One huge mistake made by actors is trying to create a photo that looks completely different than the actor's day-to-day appearance. Unfortunately, an actor whose picture is not "him" may not be identifiable by the picture at auditions. The headshot may look great, but it doesn't leave the strong or memorable impression you want because it doesn't "match" your true appearance.

Makeup for Your Photo Shoot

Many actors hire a makeup artist to attend the session with them so that they do not have to bother with keeping their hair fixed or retouching their makeup during the shoot. However, as an actor, it is important that you know how to control and manage your look without help. With training and practice, you can master the art of hair and makeup and duplicate your headshot look for auditions. As a result, the look flows smoothly from home to an audition and back again. Ask your coach if he or she can recommend a local professional makeup artist or stylist who offers makeup lessons.

> **Lar Says...**
> A model's and photographer's secret weapon: Genie Instant Line Smoother is a clear cosmetic that goes on clear, dries clear, and in about two minutes fills in fine lines and wrinkles and reduces bags and puffiness. Wear it under makeup to make your skin look flawless.

For actors younger than thirteen, avoid any noticeable makeup in headshots.

If you are over sixteen years old and wear makeup on a regular basis, simply apply your natural, everyday look just as you would if you were going on a date or a job interview. That would mean using a cover cream, powder and a light lip tone on the lips – no heavy gloss. Use minimal application of mascara and curl eyelashes as needed. For modeling fashion shoots, heavier makeup will most likely be required. Remember, you want to be natural, but also "special." I would advise that you either talk to your coach or see a makeup artist if you are unsure how to apply your makeup properly. Your goal is to strive for a "real" you, not a "made-up" you.

Avoid "free" makeovers at department stores for the price of a cleanser or lipstick unless you are looking to purchase cosmetics. Make-up artists at cosmetic counters tend to use much heavier makeup, and the colors are normally applied too intensely for an actor's headshot. Their goal is to sell *their* product, and your goal is to sell *your* product – **You!**

If you do not have a coach or trusted industry mentor on hand, contact a licensed union agency in your town and ask them for makeup artist referrals. If they do not have a make-up artist list, ask for a headshot photographer list. They should not have a problem giving you a photographer's referral list. How will this help? Photographers have a list of makeup artists they work with regularly. This will require some investigative work on your part, but the outcome is well worth the effort.

Differences Between a Model's Portfolio and an Actor's Headshot

As mentioned previously, a model's portfolio, or book, is a collection of photos which are more fashion-oriented. While I believe modeling and acting are merging together more than ever, there are still differences the industry expects and, *in fact,* demands.

Models need a nice headshot, three quarter, and full-length shots. Unlike actors who want to wear styles as close to every day as possible, models need to shoot up-to-date fashion looks. Models are portraying "fantasy," whereas actors are portraying reality.

Models use makeup and hair and accessories to create visual stories. Acceptable model shots can be looking off to the side, posing dramatically, and detailed fashion styling. Naturally, these would not be suggested for an actor's headshot.

Building your modeling portfolio should not be a rushed event. You may have heard someone say that you can "shoot your portfolio in a day." That is one way scam artists get people to pay large sums of money. *Have an entire portfolio shot today and be a star by tomorrow.* It <u>does not</u> work that way.

A portfolio is a compilation of your print work and tear sheets gathered *over time.* You need to realize it is better to have two or three fantastic shots than to have a whole book of not-so-great ones. As you build your portfolio, you can drop the older photos.

Models usually take their entire portfolio when they have an appointment, but actors do not. Instead, an actor will have his headshot, résumé, and demo. At industry functions it is best to have photo business cards to hand out rather than have to stumble through a stack of standard 8X10 headshots.

When I coach, I am always amazed that models and actors bring me every picture that they have ever taken and call it their portfolio. This is not a portfolio; it is a *problem*. What is disheartening is that 90% of the pictures in these "portfolios" will have to go. People feel because they have put so much money, time, and effort in putting the pictures together, they need to be included. Sometimes, rearranging the photos to create a better flow can salvage a weak portfolio. However, only the best pictures should be showcased. If there is any question as to whether or not a photo should be included, it probably shouldn't. Remove it. Like an adhesive bandage, it will only sting for a moment!

Portfolios have front and back pockets you can fill with résumés and extra proof sheets. Here's a secret: the pockets are the first place industry professionals look because we know this is where amateurs and lazy talent put the materials they do not want us to see. Only include your best material in your portfolio – pockets and all!

Be aware of common mistakes like these as early as you can and avoid them. If you do not have great pictures for your book, re-shoot. Learn from your mistakes and move on. Businesses are not built in a day and your career is your business!

Editing Your Photos

After completing your session, it is time to edit the photos. Most photographers set up a digital viewing station or give you a CD of the raw images. Editing is time consuming. Hopefully, you will have a team and a coach to help decide the shots to duplicate. Many photographers edit but some do not. Some will charge for edit time, while others will not. Find out your photographer's editing abilities and fees in advance, so you don't incur unexpected expenses.

You must carefully study each shot. Do a quick run through and toss any blurred images, shut eyes, or strained or forced smiles. Next compare shot to shot. Pare down and down again. When you find a few shots that look the same, carefully examine them closely for subtle differences, such as wide open eyes, relaxed smiles, and hair in place. These areas can help you to choose one photo over another. If the photographer is present or you have the capability at home, zoom in on an eye to see if the photo is out of focus.

In choosing shots from several "looks," try to pick a different facial expression in each wardrobe change. This helps you maximize the various looks you are trying to create. After selecting the three to six images, the photographer may need to do some retouching. Retouching is not about shaving years and perfecting a face. Retouching involves color correction, smoothing out the skin tone, and making subtle enhancements to the photo. When that process is completed, you will need to have the shots duplicated at a printer.

Headshots: Before and After Professional Coaching

People are wonderful and beautiful, but not every picture is. Here are some examples of how great performers can have substandard photographs and how these were transitioned into amazing headshots. No professional makeup artists were used in any of these after shots. By using basic rules of wardrobe, styling, and determining the character "type," the actor was more ideally showcased. I personally styled and directed all aspects of each of the "after" shots, including makeup, hair, expression, and energy. Now you get to reap the benefits and learn from them. A special *thank you* to each of these gracious actors for allowing their pictures to become a part of this headshot lesson.

| Sean Before | Sean After |
| Annette Before | Annette After |

(See color insert for more examples.)

An Expert Says…

Getting That Winning Headshot

Brad Barton, Headshot Photographer
www.txheadshots.com
www.b2pix.com

Your headshot is the most important item you have for marketing yourself. Ninety-nine percent of the time, the face that is looking out from that piece of paper is the first impression an agent or director will have of you; and as the saying goes, "You never get a second chance to make a first impression." When a casting call goes out, they may receive hundreds of different headshots in the mail. The casting directors will spend, on average, about one second per image as they sift through the pile of envelopes. If your headshot doesn't leap off the page, it may never be looked at again.

So how do you make a first impression that impresses?

- **Go to a photographer who specializes in headshots.** I cannot stress this one enough. A portrait is not a headshot. You can take a fantastic portrait that your mother will adore, but it may not get you in the door on a casting call. Why? For the most part, portraits are about lighting and backgrounds and posing. Headshots are more like a product photo you see in a magazine, only your face is the product. Portraits are made better by heavy makeup, jewelry, and the sweater you got for Christmas. Headshots are made better by simplifying, by removing the jewelry, by avoiding the heavy makeup, and by choosing clothing that draws attention to the face, not the clothes. *You never want to show up to an audition looking different than the headshot that got you the audition.*

- **Make sure your photographer is willing to give you unlimited printing rights.** Most portrait studios make their money by selling you prints, not by selling you the portrait session. These studios generally are not willing to grant you unlimited printing rights without charging you a great deal of extra money for it. It's a classic bait and switch scam. They lure you in with low session fees and then surprise you with after session markups. *Make sure your photographer knows you need unlimited printing rights and that it and all other costs are included in their price.*

- **Learn to act in front of a still camera.** Please note that I did not call it "posing." You are an actor, not someone sitting for a portrait. Every expression you have when facing the camera should have a thought behind it, a motivation to make it. Your eyes should portray the thought and the emotion as much as your face. There is nothing that puts a headshot in the cut stack faster than lifeless, emotionless eyes. You need to be able to wake up your face on a moment's notice through a thought (find your motivation in the look you are shooting) or an action (shaking the head or arms and fingers in order to loosen up). A good photographer who specializes in headshots can help you with direction, but you cannot count on them for motivation. *Perform for the camera just as you would for an audience.*

- **Choose the correct wardrobe.** When preparing your wardrobe for a headshot session, bring a variety of solid colors and combinations that can be layered, such as a white crew neck t-shirt with a denim or leather jacket or a tank top with a light sweater. Stay away from things like logos, spaghetti straps, and busy patterns. These clothes may look good on you in person and may describe your personality, but they do not make for a good headshot. *Wardrobe needs to be well thought out, but still simple so it does not draw attention away from you.*

You and your photographer are a team. Neither one of you can produce that killer headshot by themselves. Just like your auditions, preparation is key. Find the right photographer, relax, and immerse yourself in the moment to get the shot that will get you the role.

Octavia   Robert   Sina

Ursula   Mary Jean   Kiyan

Jordan   Sascha   Suzi

© Brad Barton

CHAPTER 4

THE PERFECT RÉSUMÉ

Now that you understand the importance of a headshot, the corresponding piece of the puzzle is the résumé. Most people are familiar with the traditional corporate résumé, but there is a huge difference between this and a performer's résumé. A business résumé is 8.5" x 11" and lists education, objectives, and personal contact information. An actor's résumé is 8" x 10" (which will match perfectly to your headshot) and lists measurements, agent information, and previous acting experience.

Much like your headshot, your résumé is a key element in getting your foot in the door. Your agent submits the headshot and résumé on your behalf to casting directors hoping to secure you an audition. When you have agent representation, they may have a résumé format they want you to follow. They will give you that template, but like headshots, there are standard *Do's* and *Don'ts* when creating a résumé.

Designing Your Résumé:

The point of a résumé is to showcase what you have done and what you are capable of doing. If you have received good reviews or great quotes from any of your performances, this is the ideal place to quote them.

Your Name

This résumé is about *you*, so your name should be prominently displayed at the top of the page, *not* the word "Résumé." Your name needs to stand out. You want to use a large, bold, easy-to-read font so agents and casting directors can clearly see it. Most amateur actors use really small fonts for their names, perhaps as a subconscious way of apologizing. Fearlessly and boldly state who you are and what you have done.

Contact Information

Under your name, place union affiliations (if any) and contact information. This includes your website address, email address and a phone number.

The number listed on your résumé should not be your home number but a dedicated business line. When you get an agent, you will replace your number with your agent's number and contact information. Depending on the area of the country in which you are working, you may have more than one agent: a theatrical, commercial, and/or print agent. You will list each agent's logo. The homepage of your website will also include all contact information. Never list your home address or sensitive information like your social security number.

Vital Statistics

The next components you will need to list are your vital statistics. This will include your height, weight, hair, and eyes. You may be tempted, but do not lie about your statistics. For a child's résumé, add the date of birth (D.O.B.), but just month and year.

Acting Experience

Next, you need to include your experiences under the following categories: film, television, commercials/industrials, and theatre. There are a few differences between the East and West Coast when it comes to the order of these specific categories. Generally, the West Coast résumés would list television and film at the top of their résumé and then theatre. The East Coast résumés often list theatre at the top of their résumé and then film and TV.

If you do not have any experience, then do not list the category. It is perfectly acceptable to list student and independent films. Include extra and background work proudly. Remove these, however, as soon as you get more experience and credited roles.

Credits

There is a correct way to list your credits or to describe the part you played. They are listed across the page in three columns. Unlike a business résumé, do not use dates. Instead, put your best work at the top and work your way down to your less impressive roles. As your career progresses, start dropping background work and excessive student performances. Note that "extra" and "background" can be used interchangeably. Also, keep in mind that it is better to have a sparse résumé with strong credits than one filled with filler items of no merit.

The Proper Credit Categories

Film	**Television**	**For Theatre**
Star	Series Regular	List the title
Co-star	Guest Star	Character (and "Lead")
Support	Co-Star	Name of Theatre
Featured		
Featured extra		
Extra		

Commercials/Industrials
List the product/company
Identify if principal or extra

Special Skills

What is the importance of listing special skills? It can be a wonderful starting point for a true and earnest dialogue between casting directors and yourself. Avoid listing skills that are outdated and irrelevant to the business. Listing things such as *good with animals and children, loves shopping and hanging out with friends, or fun and easy to direct* is frivolous. These comments may have been a humorous attempt at creativity at one time, the early 1980's, but now they are overused and amateurish.

Under the special skills section, if you list dialects such as Southern, British, Italian, or others, back up that talent with a voice demo. This also needs to be a downloadable file on your website, which is an extension of your résumé. This demonstrates to the casting director you are capable of performing this talent.

It is more important to go into the audition supporting your résumé by being more extraordinary than you are, rather than to go in with an overblown résumé and not able to deliver what you say you can.

Children's Note

When listing children's credits on résumés, do not list school names. You should simply list *Elementary School, Middle School,* or *High School,* when referring to a play or performance. For your child's protection, list only the first and/or middle name on comp cards and résumés. Once a résumé is distributed, you will not have control over the people who will have access to it or how it can be used or distributed. It is always better to be safe than sorry.

Common Résumé Errors

There are several common mistakes that I consistently see when redesigning résumés:

- Incorrect paper size – the ***only*** acceptable size in our industry is 8X10.
- Multiple font types and sizes are visually distracting.
- The word "résumé" at the top of the page.
- Misspelled words and inaccurate information.
- Incorrect listing of credits and embellished experience or skills.
- Identifiable personal information such as your social security number.
- The statement "demos are available upon request" when there is no demo.
- The statement "conflicts available upon request" when there are no conflicts.

Creating your résumé is an area where you may need a professional's expertise. Skimping here may cost you in the long run. You need all of your materials to be as polished as possible.

RÉSUMÉ

JOHN DAVID

C: 214-555-8055   W: 972-555-6931 (please don't call me at work)
EMAIL: batmanfan319731@aol.com

HAIR : BROWN/AUBURN
EYES : BLUE-GREEN/BROWN
Height 5'8" (but look taller)
Weight 186 pds (I'm working out now)
DOB: 05-16-75 (AGE RANGE: 15-36)

TELEVISION

COGITO COGITO ERGO COGITO SUM   NEVER AIRED

COMMERCIAL

I WOULD LOVE TO DO SOME COMMERCIALS

TRAINING

TOOK DRAMA IN HIGH SCHOOL: GOT A B-

SPECIAL SKILLS/LANGUAGES

2 YEARS OF SPANISH IN HIGH SCHOOL, JV FOOTBALL, AIR GUITAR, GREAT
ON THE PHONE

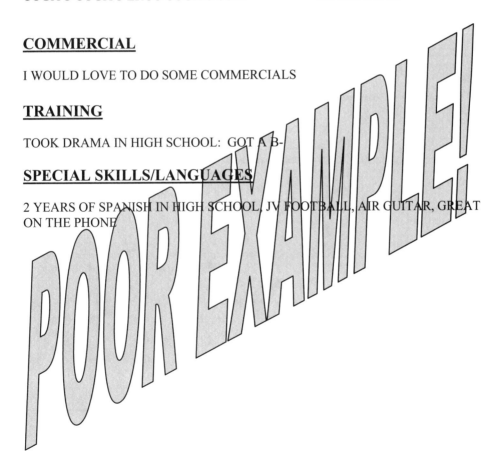

Much Better!

JOHN ACTOR

Height: 54"   **Hair: Blond**
                     Eyes: Green

972.527.3269
www.coretalent.biz

FILM/TELEVISION

Home Court Advantage	Lead	Nick Jayanty/Mind Altering Creations
Captain Freedom	Lead	Justin Hilliard/Striped Socks
With One Hand Out the Window	Lead	Rober Dahlem/Sip Sup Productions
Hate Crimes	Supporting	Tommy Stovall/PASIDG Productions
The Young Professional	Supporting	Lee Gamel/Sip Sup Productions
Reilly	Featured Extra	Greg Mansur/Caffeine Films
Barney and Friends	Featured Extra	Jillian Jester/HIT Entertainment

COMMERCIALS/INDUSTRIALS

Miller Lite	Principal/VO/National	TNK Productions

STAGE

Earth and Soul	Lead Warrior	Kids Who Care
Deep in the Heart	German Child	Kids Who Care
Giant vs Jack	Horner (lawyer)	Farr Theatre
Angel Alert	Featured Angel	Lakeside Baptist Church
Scenes From the Mall	MC	CATS, Arlington
Hotel Bethleham	Shepherd Boy	North Houston Baptist
The Rock Slinger and His Greatest Hit	David	North Houston Baptist
Scrooge and Marley	Young Scrooge/Young Bob	Main Street Theatre
Fairy Tale Courtroom	Pig 2/Sleepy(Dwarf)	Main Street Theatre
Charlotte's Web	Gosling	Main Street Theatre
Little Red Hen	Frog	School Play
Birthday Surprise	Boy Blue	CATS, Arlington
The True Meaning of Christmas	Innkeeper/Shepherd	School Play

EDUCATION/TRAINING

Lar Park Lincoln	On Camera	Dallas
Deborah Jung	Musical Theater	Fort Worth
Chris Smith Seay	Audition Technique	Dallas
Kimberly Crandall	Audition Technique	Houston
Donnajeanne Goheen	Audition	Dallas
Toni Cobb Brock	On Camera	Dallas
Will Boroski	On Camera	Dallas
Cathryn Hartt	Improvisation	Dallas
Step Rowe	On Camera	Austin
Meridith Bennett	Movement	Arlington

SKILLS/AWARDS

Boy Scout (First Class), Athletic, Soccer (9 seasons), Tae Kwon Do (Purple Belt), Percussion (Three years jazz band), A Honor Roll Student with awards in reading, science, and citizenship

Last updated 04/15/2008

An Example Using a Photo

LAR PARK LINCOLN

THE HORNE AGENCY 214-350-9220

TELEVISION

Beverly Hills, 90210	Guest Star	James Fargo, FOX
Knots Landing	Series Regular	Lorimar, CBS
Murder, She Wrote	Guest Star	Anthony Shaw, CBS
Hearts Are Wild	Guest Star	Harry Harris, ABC
Tour of Duty	Guest Star	Tommy Lee Wallace, CBS
Freddy's Nightmare	Guest Star	Tom McLoughlin, Synd
Highway to Heaven	Guest Star	Michael Landon, NBC
O'Hara	Guest Star	Bruce Kessler, ABC
Knots Landing (2)	Guest Star	K. Tilly / R. Capenella, CBS
Outlaws	Guest Star	Phil Bondelli, CBS
Hunter	Guest Star	Charles Picerni, NBC
Heart of the City	Guest Star	Donald Petrie, ABC
Children of the Night	Co-Star	Bob Markowitz, CBS MOW

Bronze Halo Award - Southern California Motion Picture Council
2003 "Gary Award" Nominee - Knot's Landing Season 91

FILM

Friday the 13th VII	Starring	John Buechler, Paramount
House II - The 2nd Story	Starring	Ethan Wiley, New World
Fatal Charm	Starring	Fritz, Kiersch, MCEG/Showtime
The Princess Academy	Starring	Bruce Block, Empire

TRAINING

Mari Lyn Henry	New York
Sam Christensen	Los Angeles
Margie Haber	Los Angeles
Jerad Barclay	Los Angeles
Film Actors Lab	Los Angeles
Bill Sorrells	Los Angeles
David Lehman	Los Angeles

ADDITIONAL INFORMATION

QVC Guest Host

Executive Producer,
Get Started Not Scammed - A Beginner's Guide to Acting and Modeling
Video / DVD, Book release 2008 - Ooh La Lar Productions

Demos Available on www.LarParkLincoln.com

CONTACTLAR@LARPARKLINCOLN.COM

WWW.LARPARKLINCOLN.COM
WWW.TALENTSTART.NET

REVIEWS

"An indisputable dazzler."
-Soap Opera Digest

"Stunning new leading lady."
-Splice Magazine

"I want to tell you that you are terrific in the show and to personally thank you."
-Aaron Spelling

"I've seen sensational dailies from you - wonderful, scary, expert performances, thank you for your talents and your efforts."
-John Romano, Lorimar

The cast is speckled with marquee magnets - the most prominent being Lar Park Lincoln."
-Bill Hagan, Film Theatre Critic

"It's Tina's (Lar Park Lincoln) movie."
-Director John Buechler,
(Friday 13th Part VII)

An Expert Says...

Headshot ROI (Rate of Interest) Rule

Bob Fraser, Author: "The Importance of Headshots" and "Bad Headshots Can Cost You Your Career"
www.YouMustAct.com

People who do direct mail advertising expect *at least a 4% return*. If they don't get a 4% return, they change the ad. Your headshot and résumé is a direct mail promotion. If you are not getting at least a 4% rate of return on your mailings, you need a new picture. For example, if you send out 100 pictures and do not receive four calls, a new headshot is probably in order.

If you are not getting good results with your mailings, here are four hints that might make your response rate more to your liking.

1. *Do not submit for auditions which are not right for you.* Do not waste the casting director's time and always be nice to them as they have a hard job. However, submit for every role you are right for and do not be lazy about it.

2. *Do not seal your envelope.* Tuck the flap in and ship it. Another good idea is to try these new "see through" mailers.

3. *Make sure that your contact phone number is answered at all hours.* If they cannot get in touch with you, you will not get the work. Get a cell phone. Pay the bill. This is a business.

4. *Your headshot must look exactly like you.* If you send a picture to a Casting Director and you get called in and you do not look like your headshot, you automatically lose the audition. However, if your picture looks exactly like you and they call you in, then you are what they want. Now that you're in the door, all you have to do is 'blow them away' with your audition.

Do your own "due diligence." A good photographer is as important as a good doctor. Do not hope to get a good result with a half-hearted approach. Your headshot is the most important tool you have. If you don't have a good one (one that gets you auditions) all your other efforts will not have the desired outcome.

A good headshot is the doorway to where you want to go.

- *Spend what you can.*
- *Work hard to do your part right.*
- *Keep trying.*
- *Keep reminding yourself, "This is the way in the door."*

A good headshot is how you will meet every casting director, agent, director, and manager in the business, not to mention their assistants and staff.

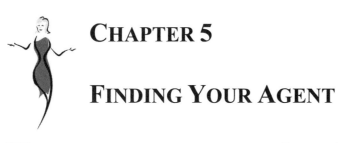

CHAPTER 5

FINDING YOUR AGENT

What are agents, managers, and coaches?

Agents and managers are alike in many aspects, but there is one noticeable and legal difference between the two. Agents negotiate contracts and handle your employment while managers "spin" your image and offer their professional advice on career advancement. Managers will play an important part in your career, but they are not necessary when you first begin. At the start of a career, if you are a parent, you are in effect your child's manager. Agents, managers and coaches have different legal, moral, and ethical responsibilities.

Your coach is the primary acting teacher. Some coaches will help you in other areas of your career and others will not. It is extremely helpful if the coach is someone who is actively working in the business. Take advantage of the experience your coach has and use it to help catapult your image and career to new heights.

Legitimate Agencies

Agents are people who represent talent for a commission. They are neither magicians nor miracle workers. They are talented professionals who excel at brokering deals. They do not usually act, direct, write, model, or produce; however, they may have done so in their past. Their primary mission is to connect actors with casting directors. Getting an agent can be just as hard as getting an acting job; make sure you take it seriously.

An agent can help you become a success, but it will still take the two of you working together to make it happen. Here are the *basics* of what an agent does versus what you need to do.

Your Agent's Job	Your Job
Submit you for auditions	Do your own submissions
Get feedback about auditions if available	Keep training
Negotiate your deals	Check in with agent weekly
Update contact information on their website	Keep materials current and obtain copies of work
Agents get a percentage of your fee in commission	Keep track of tax deductions

Steps to Obtaining an Agent

There are some steps you can follow that will make finding an agent easier. Start by going to *www.SAG.org* or your state licensing board for an up-to-date listing of agents and additional useful information.

Step 1:
Investigate the Agency's Credentials

As you navigate the various agencies, verify each one's credentials. It is important that an agent is listed with the Screen Actor's Guild and the Better Business Bureau. *A licensed agent must be registered in the city, county, and state of their business.*

Step 2:
Contact the Agency

Most agencies require you to mail or email them a headshot, résumé, and demo to request representation. They also may have an "open call" day on when you can meet the agent in person. Follow the agency's submission requirements very carefully. If you follow them exactly, you will be ahead of most other submissions.

If interested, an agency will usually respond within approximately four weeks, but there could be a number of reasons an agency does not respond to your submission. Perhaps they neglect their mail. It could be that they have too many submissions or are not looking for new talent. It is even possible that they have been on vacation.

The unfortunate truth is probably that they are not interested in representing you at this time. Do not let this get you down. Hopefully, there will be more agencies who will want to represent you.

In the event that you have contacted every agent in your area and received no response, do a second submission. If there is still no response then it is time to do a business analysis (you are your business). You may need re-evaluate your type, redo your headshots, book a consultation with a coach if you have not already done so, and then resubmit to the agencies.

There are many reasons an agency cannot or will not accept any one at any given time.

- They may already have several clients similar to your type.
- They have an adequate talent pool at the time.
- They do not feel you have the experience they need.

What happens when you submit your headshot to an agency?

When you submit your pictures to an agent, one of several things will happen:

1. They will fall in love with your headshot and call you immediately for a meeting.
2. They will dislike your shot and you will never hear from them.
3. They will love your shot and still never call you.
4. They will call you for a meeting, like you, but dislike your pictures.

The agent may ask you to:
1. Get training
2. Grow taller
3. Get braces on or off
4. Change your hair
5. Shoot more headshots and resubmit
6. _____ fill in the blank

At this point, you would need to make a decision on how much time, effort and energy you wish to invest in your career.

Step 3:
Your First Meeting

Hopefully, an agent *will* call you and ask to set up a meeting. Minors must have an adult present. Do not take friends with you in hopes that "Hey, maybe they will take you, too!"

Get to the meeting ten to fifteen minutes early, but be prepared to wait. Agents are very busy, and although they may have initiated the meeting, it is still more important for them to book their current clients than to stop everything to accommodate you.

Do not get upset if your prospective agent is on the phone 75% of the time you are in the meeting. In fact, be worried if they aren't! Agents do not have the luxury of having someone "hold their calls." They must be prepared and ready at any time to book jobs and schedule go-sees.

> **WARNING:**
> Valid agents do not ask for a registration fee, but some do ask for an annual maintenance fee to include the talent on their website. Your agent earns a small percentage as payment *after* you book a job.

If the agent gives you a contract, read it over carefully before signing. The moment will be exciting, but it is more important to make sure you understand the fine print than to find yourself trapped in an agreement because you felt rushed. Contracts with agencies are usually simple. There is generally a thirty day "out" clause, which means either of you can decide to end the relationship with thirty days notice to the other party.

An agent does not want you if you do not work, and you do not want them if you are not working. No hard feelings. It is not personal. NEXT! You will change agents throughout your career. This is normal. You may be with an agent for years before booking a job. As long as your feedback is good, and call back ratio is high, the agency will usually continue to represent you. Remember, it is up to you to develop a good agent relationship. If you are not consistently auditioning and booking, it may not be your agent's fault. Before searching for new representation, give your current agent the opportunity to market you with updated marketing materials.

At your meeting, you may be asked to either read some commercial or theatrical copy or bring a prepared monologue. If you already have a professionally edited demo reel, be sure to bring that with you and be prepared to *leave a copy*. If you are called in for an interview after submitting a headshot and demo reel, bring extra copies of your headshots with you.

When meeting with your prospective agent, you will both be interviewing the other, so be prepared. Your agent should be excited about you, and you should be enthusiastic about him or her. You should ask a list of questions that are important to you. A sample list may include:

1. Who have you represented in the past?
2. Who are you representing now?
3. What kind of "type" do you think I am?
4. What will you need from me to get started?
5. How can I help *you* help *me*?
6. How many agents / assistants are working in the office?

Step 4:
Continuing the Relationship

After you have completed your interview, give yourself a pat on the back. A strong relationship with your agent is an important step in this industry. Do your part to ensure this relationship remains a positive one. Always do the following:

1. Send your agent an updated headshot and/or comp card every 6 months.
2. Be sure your agent has an adequate number of headshots and résumés on hand.
3. Send your agent a postcard whenever something happens in your career.
4. Gather as much acting or modeling experience as possible.
5. Do not call your agent to see if you booked a job. If they do not call you, you did not get it.
6. Never stop training. Do what you can to improve your skills.
7. Self-promote. Do not be afraid to market yourself.
8. Mail "photo postcard thank you notes" to casting directors you have met.

> **Lar Says...**
> Remember in our business, phone time equals money. Calls are fast, to the point, and over. They are not social calls. When making phone calls, whether the person on the other end is a receptionist, agent, photographer, or anyone else, be professional. Learn to politely tend to business and then get off of the line! Don't be offended by what may seem to be a "curt" reply or answer. It's not personal. It is how business is done.

9. Do not pester your agent for feedback. Any feedback you get may have gone through several people and may not be directly related to you at all! If you push for feedback, your agent may give you a "generic standard answer." Generally, casting directors or directors will tell you on the spot if they have information for you that they think will be beneficial.

10. It is *your* job to make sure your agents have marketing materials that are consistently updated.

The Union

Many actors, directors, producers, and agents have worked hard for years to create a union that protects those working in this business and to provide benefits for them during, and after, their career. For example, the Screen Actors Guild has a pension and health plan. Members can get group health insurance if they have met certain requirements, and they may also qualify for a pension much like that of an employee pension plan and similar to working a corporate job for twenty years. That's a good thing, because it means as you mature and have put in the required years, hours, or projects, you will accordingly have retirement income.

> **Lar Says...**
> Becoming a SAG union member is an exciting step in any actor's career. However, joining can be a financial burden even after you've met the requirements, because the initial dues are often in the thousands of dollars range.

Getting an agent can seem very complicated, but it *is* possible. All actors start out as non-union. There are strict requirements to become a member of the Screen Actors Guild or SAG. Visit www.SAG.org for specific criteria for union membership.

To get a list of agencies approved by the Screen Actors Guild, simply call the SAG, or look it up on their website at www.SAG.org. They will send you a list of the licensed, franchised agencies in your area. .

Your agent will be able to tell you the requirements in your state for getting a child's working permit for the industry. It's exciting to finally get that permit, see your name on it, and see the word actor written or stamped across it!

Where does a public relations firm fit in?

An average public relations (PR) firm costs $1500 to $5000 per month usually based on a 3-6 month contract. When you have a project such as a role in television or film that is large enough to warrant publicity, you will hire a PR firm. They will write press releases and submit them on your behalf to newspapers, magazines, and talk shows. This is an expensive and ongoing process that is used by performers to capitalize on their success and become household names. This is not for someone just starting out. However when you get a great role with established directors, producers or stars, capitalize on it and hire P.R!

Lar's First Agent Experience

Pure persistence landed me my first agent. I was initially turned down eight times before finally being accepted. I simply was not right for that particular agency at the time, but it didn't stop me from attending seven open calls in a row! I presented a different "test" headshot each time. The agent told me week after week, "We represent a certain kind of client here for a certain type of work. Thank you for coming in, and I wish we could help you, but you're simply too short for the bookings we get. I'm sorry."

> **Lar Says...**
> I am often asked if this or that agent is a "good agent." My response is, "They are a good agent if you are auditioning. Even if you are not, do not burn your bridges on your exit." More often than not, you can create a better relationship with your agent with some effort on your part.

Each open call time, I would leave disappointed but resolved to show up the next week and do it all over again. I was young and naïve, but I was also bound and determined to sign with this agency, and eventually . . . I did. I signed with my first agent and got a grand total of one job, which revealed all of one eyeball. It was for a contact lens ad and I was thrilled to get it.

I was less thrilled to finally learn what the agents already knew and I didn't want to admit. I *was* wrong for that agency. I was too short, too young, and not their "type." Eventually I left that agency and signed with one who better represented me. As a result, I began going on more auditions.

My first agency was a good learning experience. To this day I credit them for teaching me the persistence I would need to survive in this challenging career.

An Expert Says...

How to Get an Agent and Ace the Interview

Cynthia Brian, The Business of Show Business.
www.CynthiaBrian.com, www.bethestaryouare.org

"There are no limits except those you create for yourself."

There are three ways to get an agent:
1. Be introduced through a friend who already is represented by this agent or be referred by a casting person or producer.
2. Invite the agent to a play or production in which you have a lead role and hope that the agent is pleasantly impressed with your work and wants to represent you.
3. Find out which agents are franchised by SAG and AFTRA. Send these agents a short cover letter requesting representation along with a résumé with your current 8x10 color headshot Don't send out photographs that you want returned, as agents are busy and don't have time to sort through the mail to determine what needs to be returned. Make sure you have included a phone number and email address where you are reachable. Expect to wait two to eight weeks for an answer.

Most actors get their agents by using scenario # 3. Agents are careful about only representing talent that they feel are bookable at this time. This doesn't mean if you are rejected by one agent, that another agent won't want you. Keep submitting until you find an agent who is willing to give you a personal interview. When you do get an interview, remember that appearance and good grooming are very important. You only have one opportunity to make a first impression. Hair, face, clothes and shoes must be clean and appropriate. Wear clothing that makes you feel comfortable. Do not be too dressy. Do not wear jeans and a T-shirt. Do not try to look sexy. Look professional, casual, and commercial-like. You want the agent to be thinking about projects to cast you in, not where you purchased your clothes.

Beauty is not that essential. What is important is your personality and high energy looks that come from being healthy and happy. Look like the photograph you sent in the mail. You were called in because of your look on the picture; make sure that photo represents you NOW. All the materials you will need to present yourself as a professional are your responsibility, including your photographs, résumés, and demo reels.

Bring with you any pertinent information, such as a portfolio of headshots or a voice or acting demo. Do not bring in family snapshots or a home video of a recital or production. Be prepared to answer the most asked question in the business: "Tell me about yourself." Be passionate and succinct.

Once the agent has agreed to represent you, don't sit back and wait for the phone to ring. You have to take responsibility for your own career. Be informed. Get into workshops, sharpen your skills. Also, follow up with a photo post card thank you note.

In order to be successful, you will need to have a good working relationship with your agent. Many actors are under the impression that once an agent is secured, that the actors' work is finished and that the agent will do it all. NOT TRUE! It is essential for the actor to market voraciously and to keep in contact with the agent. Promote yourself and let your agent know what you are doing to further your career. If you should be contacted directly from a casting person or producer for a job, call your agent and have your agent negotiate the deal. Having your agent negotiate for you usually gets you bigger fees. I once was booked on a print job for three hours that I had anticipated charging my usual $200 per hour. When I asked my agent what she had negotiated, she said $2500 for the three hours! Obviously I was delighted and surprised. This was a definite indication of the power of the negotiating skills of my agent.

Now go out into the world and be the star you are!
Best of success-break a leg!

No matter how great your photo shoot may be, do not be offended when your agent decides they do not like it. Take it in stride, just deal with it, and remember that everyone has a different opinion.

Jack Turnbull, Actorsite.com

CHAPTER 6

AUDITIONING, CASTING, AND TRAINING

Auditions are both the bane and the blessing of an actor's existence. You will love them and you will hate them, you will hate *loving* them and love *hating* them. Auditions can be nerve wracking, stomach tearing, and excruciatingly tense. However, this is the adrenaline rush all performers crave. You need to learn to love the audition or this business will be very difficult for you.

Auditions are the bread and butter of an actor's career. In some ways, they can be seen as obstacles presided over by "gatekeepers" whose job it is, or so we think, to keep us out of the profession we love. On the other hand, they can be seen as golden opportunities, star-making moments in which to share our talent with those who matter in this industry.

Which way do you look at it? Honestly, it may change from day to day. If you are anything like me, you will soon be addicted to auditions and with good reason!

Getting the part does not always have to do with being the best actor in the room. As you become more experienced, you will understand this concept. Auditions don't happen in a vacuum; they happen in office settings with producers, casting directors, investors, publicists . . . you get the idea. Auditions are not comfortable like the calming, supportive environment of an acting class.

Personalities sometimes clash, and money is on the line. Auditions are not the time or place for you to air your dirty laundry, wear bold fashion statements, or spout political diatribes. You do not walk into an audition and step onto your soapbox about modern film versus the classics or film versus digital. Talk less, listen more, and you'll be well on your way to making a good impression.

Audition Tips

Do not be late to your audition or callback! Most auditions are spaced 3-5 minutes apart! Don't make the casting directors track you down. You have a phone. If you are going to be late, call your agent. Many cities are now starting a "list" of consistently late talent – casting directors notice, and they talk.

What is the most important step to remember when meeting someone and/or introducing yourself?

Smile and look them in the eye! They want you to be "the one" so they can stop looking and start shooting the project.

How should you shake hands?

Do not initiate a handshake with a casting director as they are meeting people all day long. However, if a hand is extended to you, you should immediately extend your hand using a firm handshake while looking them in the eye and smiling. If you are prepared, there will be nothing in your right hand so you are free to respond easily without fumbling.

How should you stand when speaking?

Always try to stand tall. Do not wiggle. Hold your hands and arms still. Remember casting people are not just watching you read your lines, but also how you walk in the door, greet them, stand, and behave. You must practice at home and on camera to master these seemingly simple techniques. We all have gestures we need to control, such as tapping feet, fidgeting hands, licking lips, or scratching your head, arms etc. A good coach can help you learn to control these mannerisms.

How do you introduce yourself?

Auditions start with the practice of a "slate." You'll find the full definition in the terms section. It is important to say your name clearly. Practice! Some of us have long names and when we say them, we mumble. In slating, it may help you to separate your name for clarity. Example "Hi, I am Austin, Austin Podowski." If your name is unusual or long, this may help them better understand you when the audition tape is reviewed later.

What should you carry into an audition?

Do not have *anything* in your right hand when you walk into an audition or interview. Keep your right hand empty and available for being introduced. Do not "dig" through bags and brief cases to get to your headshot and résumé. Have these items out, pre-stapled and ready to hand over. Carry them in your left hand. Put your keys, phone (turned off, *not* on vibrate) in a pocket or keep them outside the audition door.

***ALWAYS* BRING TWO OR THREE ADDITIONAL HEADSHOTS AND RÉSUMÉS TO AUDITIONS AND CALLBACKS.**

Headshots and résumés are not kept on file. The initial headshot and résumé goes to the director who does not always have them on hand for the auditions. Saying: "I didn't think I needed another one," is a bold statement of inexperience. It is your business card; why would you not have one with you?

Avoid being overly friendly.

Do not hug or otherwise act "familiar" with the casting people, even if you know them outside of the audition. A pleasant and warm "Hello" is enough.

BE POSITIVE!

Avoid being negative. Examples of a negative comment are excusing yourself for being late or not having looked over the material. Begin on a positive note and that includes a smile!

Never carry food or drink in your hand into the audition or interview room.

Manners have become very sloppy and this shouldn't even have to be said, but please do not chew gum or candy at an audition. Also, remember that this is a business, so avoid carrying on conversations with others in the waiting area. They are actors, like you, and are concentrating on their lines. They do not need or want to be disturbed.

How should you behave?

Do not drop by the casting studio to request a different audition time. Do not call for directions. Do not bring your entourage with you. Any appointment changes or questions about the script need to go through your agent.

Parents need to watch children at all times. Teach younger actors to be quiet and respectful at all times and at all phases of the audition sequence.

Put your best face forward.

Check your hair and makeup **outside** the door, or ask to use a restroom. Primping in front of the others is considered unprofessional.

During the actual audition when you are reading from your script (also called "sides"), keep the following in mind:

- Bend your arm at the elbow. Keep the elbow/arm touching the body bent at an approximately 90 degree angle so that the sides can be held high enough in <u>front</u> of you that you're not moving your head "back and forth" in a distracting manner.

- Keep your script level. The last thing you want that piece of paper to do is be distracting. It should be part of your performance, not detract from it.

When is the audition over?

Your audition is not over until you are in your car on the way home. Do not comment on your performance in the audition room. Do not say how bad or good you think you did. Avoid "hanging around" and distracting those waiting to audition. Just leave cheerfully and confidently. Explore the emotions of the experience only when you are in the privacy of your home.

Auditioning With Children

There is a demand for all kinds of children who are photogenic. This doesn't mean just *typically beautiful* children. There are different shapes, different sizes, different minorities or ethnic groups, small, tall, short, thin, plump – all different types of children, and they all can have a place in entertainment.

Understand that you are the main reason, at this point, that your child will succeed. As they mature, they will have to learn to run their business themselves. If you are doing your job well, you are teaching them as you go. Even young children can learn the importance of attaching headshots, résumés, and sharpening pencils. But in the beginning, it's up to you. Your role is to be available to take your child where he or she needs to go, both emotionally and physically.

Success at auditions is achievable. Employ the same strategies you might use when taking your child to any quiet venue. For example, be sure to bring snacks along with quiet toys to keep his or her attention under control during waiting periods.

My daughter started in the acting world at the age of eight months. She was a crawling baby in many commercials and continued working throughout her teenage years.

Auditioning was treated as a positive experience. The goal was to improve self-esteem, not damage it. It didn't take long for us to discover that careful planning was the key to auditioning with children.

If your child becomes a behavior problem in the casting waiting room, he or she probably doesn't want to be there. You may not be doing yourself or your child any favors by staying. Pressuring your child to do something he or she isn't interested in simply because *you* want it is inexcusable.

After the audition, if your child will be returning to school immediately, give him or her a couple of minutes to "decompress." Auditioning can be intense, and they have been on their best behavior for many hours. Take your child to a playground or to have a healthy lunch before returning to school, or allow him or her to sing out loud to a favorite song while you drive. A child needs an emotional and physical outlet – like recess – before returning to the structure of the classroom.

Should your child book a commercial, think about the impact the product will have on him or her during the long hours on the set. For example, my child did a commercial with a teddy bear, but she was not allowed to keep it because it was a prototype. She had become very attached, so letting it go was not easy. At that time, I remember wishing I had brought a toy or treat with us to distract her as we walked away from her cuddly new friend.

Little children have emotions adults have learned to control over the years. Because they do not understand fully the connection to working and getting a paycheck at a later date, a token of some kind can be a great way of letting them know they did a wonderful job.

How the Casting Process Works

> **Lar Says...**
> If you are training consistently and not getting results, there is a problem and a simple solution: You need a different coach. Do not allow a coach or acting teacher to psychologically trap you in classes that don't empower you to move forward.

After you have your headshot and résumé, you begin the process of submitting for auditions. You may be self-submitting, or you may have an agent that submits on your behalf.

A go-see simply means you need to "go see" someone. It is an appointment in the modeling world. The equivalent of this word for an actor is known as a "general". These are introductory meetings lasting a few minutes. During this time, the casting director will review your headshot and résumé, ask a few questions, and may or may not have you do a cold reading audition.

The best time for a general is during downtime when the industry is not as busy. Pilot season is **not** a good time for generals. Pilot season is when television shows are looking for their talent for upcoming series.

The actor who books the job is not necessarily the best talent, but he could be the actor with the best technical presentation or the best look for the role. Acting teachers may say technical skill is not as important as character study. I believe it is. The proof is in the booking. You can take scene study and character development indefinitely, but if you do not learn to do the technical skills needed for an on-camera audition, you will not get the role.

You may wonder why industry professionals cannot see through technical inabilities to the skills you know you possess. The people in the audition room can; however, they are not always the people who make the decisions. It is common practice to put auditions on tape. Casting directors send the audition tapes to the directors, producers, and others who will view it (or a few seconds of it) and decide whether to bring you in for a second, third, or fourth callback. The director and/or producers watch all the people who have been taped at the auditions. These tapes are used to narrow down actors for potential roles. The production office will let the casting director know immediately if there is someone they are interested in seeing for callbacks.

At your audition, understand that the camera is rolling before you begin speaking, so casting sees the part on the tape where you are fidgeting, trying to find your mark, or appearing awkward. They do not have time to watch the whole tape and watch you fumble through the first three-fourths of a poor audition, and they certainly do not have time to teach you technique. Although both casting and directors may see promise in your performance, they may think you are not well-trained. Because of their investment, they will find someone just as good but who also has good technique.

Casting directors do NOT have to be watching you to "understand" your audition. If you notice this and feel slighted, realize they will be watching the tape later. ALSO, realize you cannot be a first rate performer and an observer of what is going on elsewhere at the same time. Good preparation and being present in the moment will go a long way toward improving your audition.

The best thing to do is to be sure you know exactly how to nail your audition. Walk into the room confidently with the requested number of headshots and résumés and let your preparation and talent shine.

Follow through after an audition, go-see, or general is just as important as what you do before and during your audition. The follow-up is both your agent's and your job. Mail a "Photo Thank You" postcard immediately. This is time consuming, but it is necessary. Agents will follow up with phone calls to the casting director to get feedback. This may or may not be relayed back to you.

ARE YOU PERFECT FOR THE PART?
ARE YOU "THE RINGER?"

There are many variables that go into choosing the final cast members. If the casting director is asking for 5'4" brunettes with fair skin and your agent sends you, a woman of color or a six foot blonde, do not fret and look around the waiting room thinking you are "all wrong." You're just a ringer. That's a cool thing! This means your agent was able to get you in despite the specs or the casting director requested you specifically. At the beginning of the casting process, they may not have a clear picture of the character they need. You may be the exception – I WAS!

A good example of this is when I was brought in to read for *Knots Landing*. I was originally brought in to read for Donna Mills' character as a flashback to play her at sixteen. It was a small role, a nice part, and of course, who wouldn't want to play someone as gorgeous and talented as Donna Mills?

When I got to the audition, however, I noticed that there were five million gorgeous actresses who would be perfect for the role. I did not get that part.

Instead I went in and they asked if I would mind reading for another role. As fate would have it, it was the part of Linda Fairgate. She was supposed to be 5'9" and brunette. We all know how *that* ended up! I booked a bigger role than I was originally brought in for. Being the "ringer" opened up my options and helped to solidify my career.

Do not overanalyze why you were brought in to audition. Here is another example. An actress got an audition for a role in a Movie of the Week on a great network. She didn't feel the character was "her." She improvised about how the character should be played based on how she was described on the breakdown sheet (at the beginning of a casting process, roles and characters are described for initial submissions; this is called a *breakdown*).

This knowledgeable and experienced actress knew better, but she prejudged the material anyway. The audition came and went, and she did not get the part. She would later watch the movie and notice the similarities between herself and her technique and the appearance and technique of the actress who won the role. She had overanalyzed the material and questioned casting's desire to bring her in. She spent too much time trying to fit what she thought they wanted. It was painful to learn that all they really had wanted was her. This is a perfect example of the casting directors knowing the type of actress they wanted for the role and an actress talking herself out of a role she did not think she fit. And as embarrassing as that story is – *it was me!*

This is not to say that we shouldn't try to stretch ourselves and do unique and interesting characters. Be careful not to pre-judge or guess their intentions when a casting director invites you to come in on an audition <u>even</u> when you think you are not right for it. You just never know. They could have written the role with you in mind or want to see you "read" for another role or project.

Being prepared is more important than trying to compete against everyone else. If you are gorgeous, you may not book the role simply because you are prettier than the leading lady, too tall, or . . . well, you can fill in the blanks. You may remind a producer or director of a horrible ex-spouse or some other bad experience.

So do your audition and then forget about it and go on to the next. Remember, the feedback you receive on any audition needs to be taken with a grain of salt. They may not be accurate representations of your acting ability. In acting, it is not always about you.

A Day in the Life

Recently, I received a call that would put into motion a series of career altering events. It was an audition call. Here's how the story goes.

At 4:30 pm, I received the first of six emails notifying me of an audition for an upcoming feature film at 2:05 the next afternoon. An audition, great! My agent sent me the script via email to review. The script read well and it already had some celebrity names attached to it. She also sent me the character breakdown, description, and the location of the audition. It was to be held in another city. This is not unusual for our business.

I cancelled all of my evening plans, including a date with a man who was almost certain to have been my Mr. Wonderful. I spent the night studying the script. I rescheduled childcare for pickup/delivery of my children while I was away. I warned my son that one of our large standard poodles was in heat and she was not allowed outside. The thought of 8 new standard poodle mix puppies danced around in my mind as I hoped he would heed my warning.

The next morning, I sent the kids to their separate schools and tucked the dogs neatly away. Then, with perfect clothes pressed, headshots and résumés in my bag, a copy of my script, makeup, hair supplies, cash for the road, a full tank of $3.00 a gallon gas, and a dead cell phone, I began my four and a half hour journey to the audition. I stopped to get a new cell charger before I left town. I called and begged a dear friend to take my son to baseball practice after school. It was the start of a three-day holiday weekend, but in Hollywood there are no holidays.

I arrived at my destination about the time my oldest started her last class of the day. I changed from comfy road gear to elegant audition clothing in the car. I put on my makeup and stepped out of the car a seductive character, ready to create my magic.

This was one of the nicest casting facilities in which I had been. There were restrooms, air conditioning, and plenty of seating. Auditions are not usually this comfortable. Before I even had a chance to get settled, I was called for the audition. I was given some information to make character adjustments and began my audition. 3.2 minutes later, I was out the door and on my way home. The audition went well and I had a great feeling about it. The casting director was wonderful. I gave a nice performance and I had a good reading. Callbacks were to be announced in a few days. By the time I got home, I was exhausted. Total drive time - 9 hours, 436 miles.

Notes to self upon return:

- Remember to send photo post cards to the casting director and agent for getting me the reading.
- Owe my friend yet another "dinner out" for helping with the children. Be glad that children didn't have auditions on the same day.
- Be thankful that there are no new poodles on the way!

- Need to get more CDs for car – dialect handbooks on tape, etc.-can always learn something new while driving.
- Call back possible Mr. Wonderful. See if he is free this weekend.
- Get clothes cleaned in case of callback – drop off at dry cleaners tomorrow (Starbucks landed on cream jacket as did a shade of "pick me peach" lipstick!)
- Acting class tonight.

This is but one day in the life of an actor. The "Controlled Chaos" is something performers deal with day to day in order to earn roles. You'd better be motivated!

An Actor's Toolbox

In addition to your home office, you will need to "go mobile" at a moment's notice. Picture this scenario: Your agent calls with great news. "Listen, you've got a callback for a Lifetime movie. They really liked your audition. Be at this address within the hour and ask for Susan, the casting director. She'll be waiting for you …"

Your agent calling you with one hour's notice? *Unavoidable.*

Being prepared when they do? *Professional*

It's important to be organized at all times. Actors and models are busy people; between classes, auditions, mailings, and the day jobs we need to support our first love, it's hard to find time to get organized. But that's all the more reason to GET organized

Here are other tools you will need in your actor's toolbox:
1. 8x10 paper – the industry uses 8x10 headshots that need coordinating paper résumés and cover letters. (You can cut down standard paper if you cannot find 8x10 paper, also called UK Quarto.)

2. Stapler - for keeping new sides together and attaching your headshot to your résumé
3. Staples
4. Staple remover - for taking sides apart in case of additions, deletions, etc.
5. Highlighter - to highlight your part for cold readings, auditions, call backs, etc.
6. Pencils - to take notes on your sides
7. Pencil sharpener
8. Stacking bin or file folders
9. Envelopes
    a. business size
    b. 9 x 12 manila mailers
    c. window envelopes that show the 8 x 10 photo without being opened
10. Digital camera - for when casting directors need a shot on the spot; bring it with you in case they don't have theirs

Training for the **Right** Career

Regardless of your career path – be it acting or modeling, stage or film, voice work or modeling parts – skills must be learned and mastered. Take time to plan a continuing education program for your business. Focus your training where you will get the most for your investment.

This book will be a valuable asset in your educational journey. Unlike a fussy textbook or a glossy magazine you wouldn't want to mark up, this book was designed with notes and scribbles in mind. The wide margins, big pages, and ample spacing leave you plenty of room to take notes, doodle thoughts in the margins, or highlight or check off various tasks, goals, and lists you've made. These areas are mandatory for excelling in this industry. You do not have to study all of these things at the same time nor do you have to study all of these things before you get started, but you *do* need to know about these classes.

1. Scene Study

Scene study is a must-take continuing class, whether you go into acting or modeling. You might be surprised to learn that modeling is not just standing there and looking pretty in designer clothes or posing with a product in your hand. You are a character telling a story, so scene study can be very useful in developing your skills.

Scene Study is a class that you will take for most of your career. Weekly classes vary from about three hours to much longer, depending on the teacher. Really good teachers will keep their students longer, focusing on mastery rather than the clock.

You want to study scene work with several different coaches, but not always at the same time. Let's say you study with five different scene study coaches. They're all unique, and each one is going to give you different ideas and strategies and offer insight into your work. Don't make the mistake of falling so much in love with your first scene study coach that you never move on to study with different people. You need variety; you need to study with different people. You can always have that favorite coach to go back to for private coaching for auditions and callbacks.

When shopping around for a new coach, ask if he or she will let you audit a course, which means to attend one or two sessions without charge and you can get an idea of how they teach. However, there are many advanced master coaches that do not allow audits. I do not allow audits. I feel it is disruptive to the class to have new actors constantly dropping into evaluate. You should follow your own instincts. It is much more important to know when to get out of a class that is not effective.

Pick one coach to start, and begin. Maybe you've picked several coaches or classes and you want to try all of them. It's not realistic in the beginning to study with several coaches at the same time. It's not fair to the techniques and strategies they each want to teach. Master the various lessons before confusing yourself with too many options.

How long is long enough? Study with one for 6 months, study with another for 6 months, and then perhaps move on to another, stay with the second, or go back to the first. Whatever you decide to do, scene study and cold reading audition technique are one of the first places you'll want to begin your training in this industry.

What to Expect in Different Classes

1. Scene Study Class

Usually scene classes will consist of either a small class of 10 or fewer students. However, there can be classes of up to 50-75 students in master classes in New York or California.

The purpose of a scene study class is to learn the dynamics of each character and how to define the important changes that need to occur to move the scene forward. You will usually work with a partner, perform, be critiqued by the coach and sometimes the class. Then it is common to redo the scene after you and your scene partner incorporate the feedback you have been given.

Scene study classes usually do not spend time in career goals, auditioning or the business side of your career.

2. Cold Reading Class

In addition to your scene study classes, cold reading class is extremely important. You cannot get the job if you do not audition well. Cold reading is a skill. It's a specific technique, a way of performing in front of casting directors, directors, producers and hopefully the network. Cold reading is at the *top* of the list of the basics of our business for getting a job, but in no way does it upstage the skills of acting in the first place. You can do a cold reading class and a scene study class at the same time.

Unlike scene study where you work with a partner, in cold reading you usually work as an individual. You are given a scene or monologue and 10-15 minutes to study it, thus the term *cold.* You will be taught how to diagram a scene, find the strong choices, and be confident about your choices. This class will give you the skills needed to have strong, successful auditions.

3. Film Technique Class

You also need to study a film technique class, or you can learn as you go by taking part in colleges and student films produced in your area.

The technique of film is interesting. It's technical. It means you have to explore your creative side and create characters, but you also need to understand film technique so that the camera can catch your magic. If you don't master the technique and the camera misses your performance, you will not end up on the screen.

To end up on the screen, you have to know how to study a script and develop a character. You have to learn how to work with the film crew, to understand what the marks are for, what it means when they need you to do certain types of shots, what it means to cheat to the camera, what script continuity is, and the terms used on the set.

You can be a terrific actor who has mastered cold reading and whose scene study is totally under control. However, if you don't know how to work with the film crew and technical crew on a set, chances are your face won't end up on the screen and you won't end up on next week's show.

4. Improvisation and Monologue

These are two different classes, but they complement each other. With improvisation or improv, you learn how to create scenes and characters with words, sentences, ideas, and theater and stage games. It keeps you on your toes and keeps your mind sharp. It helps you learn how to develop the more interesting sides of characters that aren't written into a scene. Sometimes the words don't portray a very interesting character on the written page, but with a well-trained actor, the character is brought to life. For terrific improvisation in acting, catch a few episodes of *Who's Line is It, Anyway?*

In the beginning of your career, you are going to need a monologue. Taking a monologue class will help you prepare one of these difficult solo pieces for agents and also for general meetings.

5. Voice Training

Add voice training to your list of classes to be studied. You will want to lose those regional accents or, on the flip side, you might need to *learn* a few accents. You must learn how to enunciate and pronounce the words that are in the dialogue the way the character would say them. You will also learn vocal control and strengthening, helping to make your voice more pleasing and easier to understand.

You will do vocal exercises, work with pitch and pronunciation as well as the pacing of your reading. You will also fine-tune your own regional accent if you have one, as it may limit your roles.

6. Dance and Body Movement

As an actor or a model, your body is what is used to convey what the character is feeling. Your face is used to create emotions, as is your body. We all know that when we're depressed, we may have our shoulders hunched or head slumped, but there are other subtle signs that you can learn and study. Your body needs to be in good shape, but this does not mean thin. Your body needs to be in good shape so that you are flexible, so that it can move and you are comfortable moving with it.

Actors must work hard to learn to have control over their bodies. This allows them to make their bodies do what is needed for the job.

Education Summary

Beginners should start with scene study and cold reading, and then go into other areas. Attend at least one weekend seminar every two to three months held by a casting director or teacher who may be traveling through your town. If you are in a major city, attend as many weekend seminars and workshops as possible.

Consider an inexpensive seminar. Be wary of those that promise work. Don't let a two-hour drive turn you away. That's just part of the job.

Education is what it takes to make it in this industry. Smart actors know how to benefit from their coaches, and they do it often. Do something, one small anything that advances you towards making your vision for your life a reality.

Although it may seem daunting, and occasionally is, the process above repeats for the rest of your career.

My Callback Ratio Has Tripled!
Arianne Martin
www.ArianneMartin.com

When I first started out, I was completely frustrated because I didn't even know where to begin! I was in an acting class and had an agent, but THEN WHAT?! I'd go out on a couple of auditions, but only a few were somewhat successful. My audition skills needed help, my headshots where only so-so and anytime I would ask my coach at the time the answer would always be, "You need to stay in my class! They'll know if you're a good actor."

B-A-L-O-N-E-Y!

Then a NEW coach came to town: Lar!

I learned so much in the first two classes than I had learned in an entire year! I learned that auditioning is a WHOLE DIFFERENT BALL GAME! And it actually does take technique. I learned how to understand "typing" yourself as an actor and using that to your advantage! I learned about marketing, websites, postcards, and business cards! Wow! It actually became a successful business as well as an art! Since then, my callback ratio has tripled, I have FANTASTIC headshots, I've been in front of some of the biggest casting directors in the South . . . not to mention some from L.A.(yeah, little ol' me from Dallas!) It all takes a little extra time and effort . . . but the results are HUGE!

An Expert Says...

It's a Numbers Game

Margie Haber, Author – How to Get the Part . . . Without Falling Apart!*, Creator of the Haber Phrase Technique® for Actors*
www.MargieHaber.com

In class, actors often ask why they should go out on a particular audition – they would never get the part, they say; it most likely will go to an actor with a high TVQ (a rating system used by broadcast television to determine a television actor's popularity and star power). Or, they'll tell me they hate the material; it's trite and superficial. Or, they can't get into the character correctly. Whenever this topic arises (and it does, with some frequency), I always remind them that auditioning is a "numbers game." An actor who goes out on twenty-five auditions and commits to the work will eventually get a job.

Every audition you go on increases your odds of winning a part; each reading gets you closer to booking a job. Actors often ask me if they should audition for a part that is not right for them and I always tell them, "Yes!" If you understand the material and can fully connect to the character, then, by all means, go for it. Go on as many auditions as you possibly can – the more, the better. (If you are in that stage of your career when your agent is only submitting you for starring roles in major films, you can be more selective.) After all, auditioning takes practice: you constantly need to flex your audition muscles to stay limber, so when the right role comes along, you'll be primed and ready to give it your best shot.

Going on lots of auditions also gives the casting people a chance to know your work. Even if you're not right for a particular part, if you give a great audition, the casting director will likely remember you and call you in for a future project – casting directors have great memories; that's part of their job. Many actors get jobs this way: an actor may go on an audition, give a great read, get fantastic feedback, but not get the job; three months later, the same casting director may call the actor on his own – without submission by the agent – for a different project.

DIFFERENT LOOKS, SAME DAY

Madison has a wide variety of looks. With pre-planning, we were able to customize one photo session and create three distinct looks: the fresh girl next door, the tough teen, and a commercial smile.

This was Shawn's first photo session. He was thrilled to be coached into creating three completely different characters in one sitting: the college student, the young businessman, and the "bad boy."

Both of these actors landed an agent within a week of these photo sessions.

LAR'S ON-SET PHOTO COACHING
BEFORE AND AFTER

In the before, Cristie's wardrobe doesn't flatter her body or create a strong impression. Her posture, leaning against the wall, is passive and her expression is forced.

Cristie

We shaped her eyebrows and had her hair chemically straightened. I chose a soft, colorful top and natural makeup. Don't you agree she looks 15 years younger?! You can also see a fun, "character shot" of Cristie on page 7.

BEFORE AND AFTER

Kevin's before shot is what I refer to as a "passive" pose. He is leaning away from the camera with his arms crossed. His tilted head and smirk give off an "I don't care" attitude. His wardrobe is bland and wrinkled.

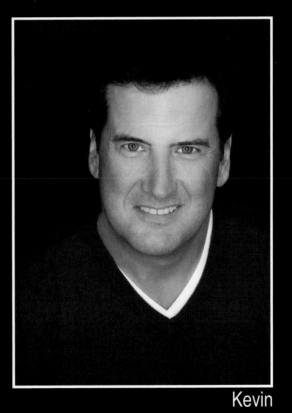

Kevin

I posed him correctly, leaning forward and "into" the shot. We layered his wardrobe using a deep brown color to offset his eyes. His open expression and sparkling eyes reveal a personality ready to be cast.

BEFORE AND AFTER

Tara's before represents a very common mistake: taking a beautiful woman and making her look average. Her posture is poor, the wardrobe and background is distracting, and her smile is nervous.

Tara

Wow! There's nothing "desperate" about this housewife. Sparkling eyes, complimentary colors, and strong posture portray her as full of energy and confidence.

BEFORE AND AFTER

James' before is not necessarily a bad headshot, but I felt he could do better.

James

For his after, we worked on creating an intensity with his eyes. Layered wardrobe and a dramatic expression lend a star-like quality to this shot.

BEFORE AND AFTER

In Holly's before, her lips are pursed tightly together which comes across as defensive. She is pulling away from the shot and does not seem approachable. There is no light or life in the eyes.

Holly

After, she has a warm, open smile, with longer, softer, face framing hair. Her eyes are bright and inviting. Her pose is engaging.

BEFORE AND AFTER

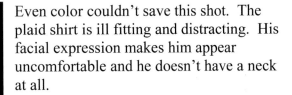

Even color couldn't save this shot. The plaid shirt is ill fitting and distracting. His facial expression makes him appear uncomfortable and he doesn't have a neck at all.

Bob

Trimming both eyebrow and nose hair, a skin care regime, a vibrant color, and complementary neckline give him the feeling of confidence, warmth, and enthusiasm. You can also see a "character shot" of Bob on page 7.

BEFORE AND AFTER

With Cherith, we have a beautiful red head, but the shot falls flat. Her wide forehead, tightly pulled back hair, and confining top are not inviting.

Cherith

Her eyes are sparkling. The makeup is natural and fresh. Her restyled and bright wardrobe bring out an energetic actress.

BEFORE AND AFTER

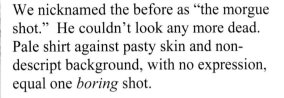

We nicknamed the before as "the morgue shot." He couldn't look any more dead. Pale shirt against pasty skin and nondescript background, with no expression, equal one *boring* shot.

Miles

After, who's this handsome guy? We highlighted his hair and we turned a lazy eye into bedroom eyes. His quiet smile is smoldering and the vibrant color wakes the dead.

BEFORE AND AFTER

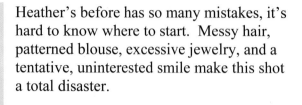

Heather's before has so many mistakes, it's hard to know where to start. Messy hair, patterned blouse, excessive jewelry, and a tentative, uninterested smile make this shot a total disaster.

Heather

Put this actress in the movies! Soft, pretty, approachable hair and full, beautiful lips complemented by the soft rose sweater with an interesting neckline make her both approachable and sexy.

BEFORE AND AFTER

Using a webcam picture is a common mistake. Poor lighting, weak smile, and dull eyes couldn't get this actor arrested.

Jason

There's a new leading man in town. Strong posture, seductive eyes, designed wardrobe, and an intense expression take this actor from not to hot.

Thank you to these professional actors for allowing me to demonstrate the difference that professional, on-set coaching can make in your photo session. Please note that for your personal headshots, you will use both your first and last names.

GREAT HEADSHOT EXAMPLES

Piper

Naima

Ashley

Tori

Angel

Melissa

GREAT HEADSHOT EXAMPLES

Eduardo   Jordan   Chuck

Jerome   James   Kiyan

These are great headshots because the actors are posed "forward," leaning *into* the shot. Genuine smiles, bright eyes, a sense of self confidence, and interesting wardrobe choices bring them to life. As you can see, a good headshot gives you an immediate and clear understanding of what kind of character type the actor could play.

FROM ACTOR TO MODEL

This was Megan's first headshot. Quite obviously, she did not understand makeup, posing, wardrobe, or expression. We see a sullen, overdone, and desperate-looking beginner.

Megan is both an actress and model, and these shots reflect that. With simply styling on the left, we have an actor's headshot that grabs attention. On the right, the shot was professionally styled in a way that kept her young, yet created the high-fashion look.

MODELING EXAMPLES

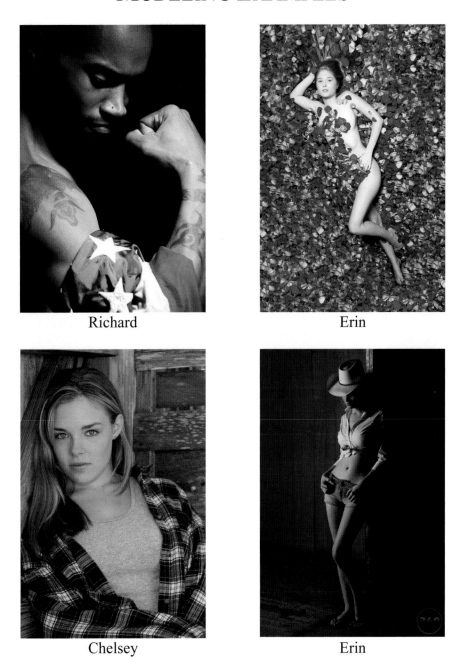

Richard

Erin

Chelsey

Erin

Here are clear examples of how modeling shots differ from acting shots. Models are more fantasy and fashion oriented, compared to the more natural and realistic headshots of actors.

RETOUCHING

On the left, Virginia's headshot has been correctly retouched. Blemishes, dark circles, makeup errors, lighting issues, and any exaggerated laugh lines have been gently softened or removed. In person, the actress would look like this picture.

On the right, while this may work for a boudoir or pageant portrait, it is inappropriate for an actor's headshot. All emotion has been erased by retouching. The hair, eyes, and teeth have all been unrealistically brightened. A photographer without experience in the specialty field of actor headshots may make these mistakes. Do not let it happen to you!

 A special *Thank You* to Virginia for allowing me to use her image for this demonstration.

PART II

Don't Get Scammed!

The reason scams work is because people are emotional, naïve, and are willing to gamble on dangerous shortcuts to overnight success.

In the second part of this book, you will learn from my years of experience how to avoid becoming victim to one of the many scams that prey upon inexperienced hopefuls.

CHAPTER 7

THE SEDUCTION OF A SCAM

Scam: a fraudulent business created to swindle money from unsuspecting people.

The reason there are so many scams in the entertainment business is because the ambition to succeed is easy to exploit. Con artists sense the desperation in actors' smiles and the passion behind their words. Location does not matter. Small towns are easy targets due to the lack of information available to them. Larger cities, like Los Angeles or New York, make desirable targets because of the thousands of hopefuls wanting to be "discovered."

A scam sets out to intentionally separate you from your wallet without getting any services in return. This is not to be confused with bad business. A bad business separates you from your money by giving you poor services or worthless information.

There are very few overnight successes. Legitimate acting and modeling careers take years to create and maintain. You must be knowledgeable about this business. You can find a grain of truth in every scam. By educating yourself so you understand the business, you are less likely to be swindled.

There are legitimate costs that accompany your acting/modeling career, as discussed earlier. If someone offers to make you an immediate success for a fee, be wary. Even though you are eager to get started, take your time and make decisions based on facts, research, and logic. If you do not, you will be easy prey for a scam artist.

Some of the ways scammers make money are:
- they earn a commission on getting you a personal "interview" or a so-called "audition,"
- they get you to sign a bogus agreement, or
- they enroll you on websites for a monthly fee or enroll you in classes or photo shoots, which are not quality programs.

To protect yourself from wasting time and money, detach from your emotions and analyze the situation. Ask yourself: What am I getting for my money? Am I spending money to justifiably further my career or am I trying to purchase a dream?

There are as many CONs as there are CON artists, and they are CONstantly reinventing their pitch. Following is a list of the most easily recognized scams divided into two sections. The first warns you about how scammers seek you. The second explains how you unknowingly seek *them.*

How Scammers Seek You

The 'Talent Scout'

"You have an amazing look! Have you ever thought of going into modeling? I work for an agency and we have an open call this weekend. It's for a major campaign in this area and you are EXACTLY what we are looking for. Here's my card, please call me so we can set up an audition."

Sounds great, doesn't it? A dream come true! Who would not want to follow up on this once-in-a-lifetime opportunity? You have been discovered and are now on your way to becoming a star. As soon as you get off the phone with all of your friends and family to tell them the exciting news, you call the number on the card to make an appointment for your audition. You hear the urgency in the receptionist's voice as she uses motivating words like *now, immediately, deadline, expires today, etc.*

These words are used because they are trying to confuse and flatter you and want you to take action without thinking. They are counting on your excitement.

These "scouts" you encounter do not actually have any scouting agreements with recognized agencies. Instead, most of them are recruiting for modeling "schools" or conventions, and they want you to think their offer has an expiration date. Once you set up an initial meeting, you will notice a shift. What begins as an interview turns into a high pressure sales presentation designed to dupe you out of thousands of dollars in photography and so called modeling and acting classes. In this harried situation, they promise fame, riches, and stardom for what seems to be a reasonable price. Don't open your checkbook as a result of their manipulation.

It's a pressure situation. You first commit to doing something you don't know much about, you then tell your friends and family. You make the trip, you're in the office, and now you are on *their* turf. You notice the walls seem to close in, and there you stand. These people are smart and very sharp. They are convincing and conniving and they know how to pick up on your emotions.

Direct Mail and Contests

"Congratulations! You have just won enrollment into an elite academy. As soon as you call this number, we will set up a complimentary meeting to introduce you and your family to our staff."

When you receive recruitment information like this in the mail, be suspicious. Where did this "company" get your name and address? Companies purchase bulk mailing lists of families and people interested in this business. Why would they be offering you, sight unseen, a scholarship to a school focusing on talent and appearance? Agencies are swamped with professional actors and models who are already working. Why would they actively search for new faces to represent through direct mail?

It is very easy to fall victim to a non-invasive approach like this one. Even if your common sense tells you otherwise, the possibility you could finally be discovered makes you want to call. Before you respond to this invitation, make sure you do your detective work. Contact your local Better Business Bureau or look online for information about the company. Proceed with caution and know who you are dealing with.

Cold Calling

"Hi! I'm so glad you're home. I'm calling you from the local Center for the Performing Arts. You have been selected to attend a wonderful seminar later this week at the biggest hotel in the city. There is no charge to attend, but if you are interested, I will need to have a credit card number on file to reserve your space."

While this may not be the exact wording you will hear cold callers will often use a variation of the above. They try to get you to attend a free meeting in order to discuss the possibility of you becoming an actor or model; but in actuality, they do not care about your talent, drive, or your passion for your craft. They are paid to get as many "recruits" as they can. You may wonder how they got your phone number and information about you if they are not legitimate.   Very simply, the companies they are working for purchase the bulk mailing list of people with certain interests. They also search mortgage companies and other bulk lists to find affluent families in a specific area. To them, you are only a dollar sign.

How You Unknowingly Seek Scammers

Magazine Ads

"You can be a famous model. Just call the number below and set up a free evaluation appointment at our prestigious school."

We all have seen these advertisements in magazines, newspapers, and phone books. You fill out a form and send it in. What's the harm? And you could get your big break!

There are two sides to the issue of modeling schools. Before you enroll in a lengthy and costly program, you need to know what you are trying to achieve. Are you taking classes for fun or a career?

Not all modeling schools are scams. In fact, I taught at one of the major modeling schools for over eight years. It was a great experience teaching beginners the world of fashion modeling, and the students loved their classes.

However, many modeling and acting schools are not legitimate. They are located in very nice, high traffic, expensive areas. They are furnished beautifully with fancy artwork and framed 8x10 celebrity headshots. The schools appear successful and attract the attention of all who enter. This is an underhanded way to lure you into feeling like they are legitimate. But looks can be deceiving. Not all of the celebrities on the walls are graduates of the program.

The instructors are usually models and actors in the city earning extra money by teaching on weekends. They are usually contracted and have no actual affiliation with the financial aspect of the school. The scam side happens when these schools cross the lines of education and focus on money making.

At one time, these schools were reputable, self–owned, and professionally operated. They became known as *the* places to go for not only modeling and acting training, but also for social and debutant skills. Over time, they became franchised businesses. With each new owner adding their own business experience and expectations, the schools often ended up developing extra departments. Often one of these new departments was a so-called "agency." Here's the catch: To be represented by this agency, you must have finished not only the beginning classes, but also various advanced programs.

A grey areas occurs when these schools hosts a "modeling convention search." They invite their students to meet with *experts* to determine if they are qualified for promotion to the next level of success. Only a handful of students are chosen to be a part of this convention, which is usually not held locally. What the students do not realize is they were not just chosen by looks or talent, but rather by their financial status or the financial status of their parents or guardian. The schools learn of the child's financial standing by looking at his/her records. They know who buys the most photos, who wears the newest clothes, who signs up for the extension courses, and which students pay their fees on time. *Anybody who can pay can attend one of these conventions!*

The most blatant financial scam used by schools is disguised as a legitimate business necessity, the portfolio. The bottom line is professional industry photographers earn their money on session fees, not prints. Schools that have "photo sessions" included in their curriculum earn profit by convincing students to purchase lots of photos at each session. You only need a couple of finished images per session, per outfit. They usually overcharge you in comparison to general industry standards.

Conventions and Expos

"You're invited to attend our convention where 'the most important people in the business' are searching for new talent!"

You may have found an ad for a convention or exposition in your area. The only problem is the most important people in the business are in

Hollywood or New York making movies or putting together fashion layouts. They are **not** at these conventions. The ad lists names that sound prestigious, but instead of meeting people who can further your career, what you really get for your several thousand dollar registration fee is a long weekend to nowhere.

Internet Agents and Websites

"Post your picture here and let the jobs find you! Hundreds of producers and casting directors search this website every day for the next new star. Make sure you're seen!"

After visiting the website, you decide it is right for you. It looks professional, the costs seem appropriate, and no one turns you down face to face. You sign up, submit a few photos, and fill out a résumé form with your statistics and information about the types of jobs you are seeking.

The first photo is free, but additional photos cost more. You are also charged to move to "higher" viewed areas of the website to give your portfolio more exposure. People post specifics on these websites with the idea that they will be seen and flown into big cities for auditions. Now you might get the opportunity to be seen on the site, but you are still sight unseen.

Usually you will have to enter a credit card number, so they can automatically withdraw money for the website's recurring fees. These websites work off of your emotions and often pressure you to sign up without thinking about the long term costs. If you decide the website is not quite what you were looking for, you may have a hard time cancelling or there may be a high cancellation fee.

If you plan to be a professional working actor or model, you need your *own* website. Do not sign up and pay to be seen on a bogus website. Spend your money to have a professional site developed that is geared toward the people in the industry. Do not include personal diaries, blogs, and family pictures. Instead, show your résumé and links that can be sent to professional casting directors. For more information, see the marketing section of this book.

There are legitimate casting websites on the internet. There are also legitimate agencies that use the internet to showcase their talent. If you are unsure of the legitimacy of a specific website, contact the Screen Actors Guild, AFTRA or your local Better Business Bureau.

Human Trafficking: A Parent's Worst Nightmare

Where there is a market for child abuse, there are people who will do anything to profit from it. These opportunists study human nature and are always working an angle. One of the ways they target children is by using pornography websites disguised as legitimate companies.

At first, these businesses appear to be casting websites in which you post your headshot to be seen by famous casting directors. Aimed at the youngest set of aspiring talent, they amplify and boast casting calls, workshops, and competitions. Then, lured into this exciting site with great music and plenty of terrific photos, teens sign up and get free modeling newsletters or tips for their career. This free information is just the "come on." Soon the teens are asked to post a photo for free or a very small cost. Once their pictures have been posted, the children are informed that their personal website has had many hits, and the "agency" wants them to come in and take upgraded photos. This can seem very exciting for a beginner without any experience.

The teenager is contacted mostly through cell phones or e-mail. After a brief and light conversation, these kids usually agree to come in and shoot a photo session. They are even asked to bring a friend or a parent. When you arrive, the office atmosphere seems busy and professional; so the parents believe it is all legitimate. Mom or Dad signs the agreement for their child to be featured on the website and to receive notices of upcoming jobs.

The young hopefuls are booked for simple runway shows and asked to model obscure fashion lines. As time goes on, your child is asked to join a special area of the site where they will make money every time someone views their photos. Supposedly, the "important people" pay a fee to access the special section of this site. After the aspiring talent has been invited to become a part of this elite area, they are sent a list of requirements. This list often includes items such as personal information, monthly fees, and additional photos. You are also informed that companies and casting people pay a fee to see only the best models. You need to shoot new photos because you will be used in bigger ad layouts and campaigns. You are asked for body shots in either swim wear or lingerie, and a few action shots showing a sporty and or a glamorous look.

The first round of photos seems reasonable. The unsuspecting talent fulfills the requirements, and begins to receive checks for more money than they ever thought possible. As time goes on, the talent and their family get quite used to the money. Over time, the young ones will be asked to start removing clothing in the sessions. Each time, more and more money is offered. Before you know it, your child's photos have been altered, sold, and downloaded all over the world, destined to come back and haunt them for the rest of their lives.

This is not legitimate modeling; this is the beginning of pornography. Agents and casting executives **do not** cast this way. This is nothing more than a depraved and corrupt site where perverts and pedophiles go to see pictures of beautiful young adolescents. You may think that this type of scam only happens to others, but no one is immune. Our children deserve to be aware of the dangers that can happen. The only way to prevent these crimes is by educating ourselves and teaching others.

Protecting Your Minor Child

Agents need a composite of various shots, including action shots such as riding a bike, swimming, sports, or a school look. To protect the privacy of your location, avoid any identifying business signs or backgrounds in your photos such as your child posing outside near an identifiable street sign. Be sure they are not shown, or crop them out before printing. Do not pose at a school where the name is visible and do not wear a school logo. Avoid posing near a car where the license plate can be seen. Predators use landmarks like these to track down your child.

Do not give personal phone numbers that go directly to your child. Use your cell phone, office number, and/or email address for contact. Do not list addresses and dates where your child may be performing. Do not list a social security number or a place of birth. Err on the side of caution, and urge your child to do the same.

Consider giving your child a cell phone. It can help him or her stay out of bad situations, keep you in touch with them, and serve as an alarm system for getting home on time. Some now have GPS to track your child. It can also be a deterrent to keep predators from harassing your child. Authorities state the best protection is to be aware and appear confident and in control. Children and teens today know how to call for help, and having that extra security is priceless.

Say NO to inappropriate photos! What determines appropriate versus inappropriate? This varies according to the child's age. Most children do not pursue high fashion modeling as it is the hardest area to break into, but those pictures are going to be the most dramatic and glamorous type. The photos will use very intense make-up, revealing clothing and suggestive poses. Sometimes the clothing is sheer and provocative. However, it is up to you, the parent, to censor the shoots. Stay away from swim wear, underwear, and suggestive poses for children, preteens, and early teens.

You are in control of your child's photo shoot. You can object at any point to poses, styles, and wardrobe with which you do not agree. You do not have to compromise your child's safety or security for success by allowing him or her to pose nude or be put in similarly compromising positions. Stand up for your child. Simply say "No."

Shoots need to be age-appropriate, and that means the body stays covered on children. In this industry, models are essentially products, and professional clients need to see that they are fit. This can be done in a variety of ways, from a youthful swimsuit with an appropriate pose to a cute crop top showing a belly button and shorts or jeans. The shot can be active, showing athletic skill, such as skating, biking, or running.

> **Lar Says...**
> It is completely appropriate for adults to wear a one-piece swimsuit under their clothing if the actor's agent tells her that casting needs to see her fitness level.

I have been on callbacks for films where the producers needed to see how athletic my body was. My agent informed me prior to the callback. I wore a one piece swimsuit under my clothing and it was no problem at all.

The facial expression is also important. Do not allow excessive overstated pouts or looks that convey something which makes you uncomfortable. Nothing is creepier than seeing a child dressed and posed in a mature, adult style.

Trust your instinct. I was coaching a group of students in a headshot photo session. A well-respected photographer had traveled to town and had chosen to do location versus studio shots. We shot in various locations around his hotel. If someone were completely new to the entertainment industry, they might have thought the whole shoot was a scam. There were no crews running around and no dramatic set. Even though it is normal to not have fancy sets, exotic locations, or dozens of assistants running around, you want to make sure that the set up is safe and legitimate.

Never allow your minor to do his or her photo sessions alone. By reading this book, you are already more prepared than most because now you know that this business is not as glamorous as most people expect. Most photo sessions are without the glitz and glam. The same goes for agencies, many of which are located in small, nondescript, low-overhead buildings. With rare exceptions, legitimate agencies do not waste money on fancy high-rise buildings, hotel ballrooms, or radio and television advertisements. They do not need to have massive open calls to find talent. They get submissions with professional headshots and résumés every single day of every single year.

Why Scams Happen

Scams happen for the following reasons:

Inexperience
Some people just do not have enough experience and the information they need is not readily available to them. While there are knowledgeable acting books on the market, they are often geared towards the people already in the industry. The majority of these books teach technique versus practicality.

Age
Children are often too young and naïve to understand that con artists will not hesitate to take advantage of a child's dreams and goals.

Uninformed Parents

Professional actors and models make this business look easy, and every parent believes his or her child "has what it takes." Parents want what is best for their children, so when a child expresses a desire to enter into this industry, families become easy prey for scam artists.

Desire

Passion for success can cloud judgment. Regardless of age and experience, when offered a chance to achieve a dream, the opportunity is hard to resist.

Illusions of Grandeur

Human nature is a funny thing. The more we see the same advertisement in respected magazines, the more we come to believe it represents a genuine product or service.

How to Spot a Scam Artist and What They Don't Want You to Know

You have just learned about the different types of scams; now, here is a list of the most common words and phrases used by scam artists in their marketing materials to mislead you. The use of these phrases does not mean the business is fraudulent, but they should raise a red flag and make you extremely cautious.

Free Evaluation

The ads say free evaluation just to get you in the door. Once you are there, they pitch a variety of services and fees. This is the classic "bait and switch." They say that their evaluation is free, but it's not.

Here are a few examples:
- A school uses a "free evaluation" to sell you a training course.
- A competition uses a "free evaluation" to approve you to enter a contest that has a high entry fee.

These are not evaluations. These are sales pitches disguised as consulting and coaching. A consultation by someone who is qualified to provide a nonbiased opinion will usually charge a fee for their services.

You have to decide NOW!

No matter how eager a legitimate agent is to sign you, no one will demand a decision immediately. Good agents suggest you "take some time to think it over," not the other way around.

The use of a star's name, as in: "Our past participants have appeared in the movie starring . . . "

Talent scouts who "name drop" like this are simply feeding on your dreams, goals, and desires to be a professional. They state their talent has appeared in various movies, magazines, and television shows. They even use the names of known celebrities in sentences to imply these celebrities are affiliated with their company.

"We have so much work for teens your age; we will take you, sight unseen."

There is no way an agency will sign you sight unseen, especially in a business that depends heavily on your looks.

"Not an agency. Not a school."

If they are not an agency or a school, what ARE they?

Other Red Flags

While it is important to read the fine print, it is also important to look at the things which are not mentioned. For example:

No website.

The Internet is no longer new. Legitimate agencies want to showcase the talent they represent. An agent without a website is like an actor without a headshot. They may be legitimate, but are you really willing to take the chance?

No agency name mentioned.

Who are they? How can you check their credentials if there is no name listed? Who is in charge? Real agents have real names and real business licenses! They have no need to change their name every few months.

> What a great subject for your book. It seems to me that almost everyone has their hands in actors' pockets all the time (photographers, teachers, agents, and now even casting directors), just fleecing young actors for whatever they can get. In L.A. presently, it's not uncommon for actors to pay 1000 dollars for headshots and upwards of 300 dollars a month for classes! I mean, has everybody gone crazy?
> -Eric Stephen Kline, FilmActorsWorkshop.com

Actors Waste Thousands on Pilot-Season Retreat

The manager didn't deliver on promised auditions! When Kari Jones emptied out her 2-year-old son's savings account to purchase a slot for a one-month pilot-season retreat in Los Angeles, the Kansas resident hoped the trip would launch her toddler's career. According to Jones, a talent manager guaranteed daily auditions and a Screen Actors Guild-franchised agent for the month. He also promised acting classes, a rental car, rides to and from auditions, and a built-in support system consisting of the dozen-plus actors on the pilot season retreat for a grand total of $3,350. Skeptical, she researched the company online and decided the program was legitimate.

"He seemed very professional and like he knew what he was talking about," she said.

During the four weeks of the trip, Jones, said, the manager failed to procure any auditions for her son. At the end of the month, he promised to reimburse her for the rental car. He never did, and the single mother swallowed the expense.

"I emptied out my child's savings account to come on this stupid fraud trip," she said.

The manager's name is not listed on the Internet Movie Database for the acting, producing, or directing credits listed on his website, nor is he listed in the Hollywood Creative Directory.

On his website, a commonly used tactic is to list "stars" and "employment" such as a "nationally known actor" who "has appeared on TV, Film and Stage for almost 30 years."

Agents are required to obtain business licenses, but there are no California laws that regulate managers.

"That's the problem — there are no requirements. You could put a desk in your house and call yourself a manager."

"It was just a crock. All of it was a crock," said a parent whose child got one audition during the retreat. "Nobody got signed."

CHAPTER 8

SCAMMED FAMILIES SHARE THEIR HEARTBREAKING STORIES

"While I was thinking about writing my Oscar acceptance speech, my sister was thinking about writing the check." Lar tells her own scam story.

As I mentioned earlier, by the time I was eleven, I had decided I was going to do three things with my life. Like any eleven year old, nothing was going to stop me. I wrote down my dreams and this simple act gave me the courage to begin my journey.

I began to look everywhere I could for information about getting into modeling and acting. With no guidebook to consult or a coach to direct me, I did exactly what any new talent would do - I looked in phone books and in magazines for modeling agents and classes. After sending away for information, I was contacted by a modeling school and asked to come in for an "evaluation."

I immediately told my family the good news. They were ecstatic and they did everything they could to help me. My mom helped me pick out an outfit and Karen, my sister, took the day off work to accompany me to my meeting.

We had a three hour drive to the meeting, but our excitement made it go by quickly. It was a very big day for me. I was nervous, partially because I was afraid they would not want me for their school.

When we finally arrived, the school was bustling with activity. Models were coming and going, each one more beautiful than the one before. Inside, even the receptionist was gorgeous. Everything about her was perfect. I could not help but wonder if she was a model. Finally, it was my turn to go in and meet my "counselor." She was stunning and beautiful. Tall and thin, she looked like she had years of experience in the industry.

After a brief introduction and a tour of the facility, we were led into her office so she could determine my eligibility. I thought she was going to decide if I had what it took to be a model, but she really just wanted to convince me to take a course at the school. I was put through an evaluation. She checked my height, weight, nails, and hair. She even asked me to walk down a mock runway so she could see if I had high fashion potential. After the evaluation, she sat me down and informed me of the things I needed to improve. The first challenge was my height. She informed me that most models were 5'7" or taller. At 5'0 tall, I had a little growing to do, but she was certain that I would grow into a perfect height.

Aside from my height problem, she also informed me that my nails needed work. She gave me some "free valuable" insider advice. She told me if I took off my nail polish, soaked my nails in olive oil, applied 5 new coats of nail polish and 2 topcoats every night, my nails would be long and strong. There was even a chance that I could become a top hand model and book all sorts of advertising work in that field. The thought of doing a manicure every night and waiting for all those coats of nail polish to dry was intimidating, but I was willing to do it.

I did not have a weight problem, but if I had, I am positive that she would have given me some kind of questionable diet to use.

After the counselor talked to me about my evaluation, she said the words I had been hoping to hear since the moment I received my invitation in the mail. "You are accepted."

I was accepted! I couldn't believe it! Once the excitement become manageable, I realized I didn't know "to what" I had been accepted.

She proceeded to tell me about the school and the classes I was now privileged and qualified to participate in. Tuition, I learned, could be paid over several years using their low interest monthly payment plan. At this point, she implied that after graduating from the school, I could be a successful model and actor. This investment in my career would be small in comparison to what I would earn once I completed the necessary courses. This woman had only spent an hour with me. She had never seen me in a photograph, and she had never seen me perform, but she knew I had "it."

While I was thinking about my first Oscar, my sister was thinking about the first payment. Karen asked all the right questions, but she was given vague answers designed to distract her from the reality of the situation and refocus on my future. Although we were offered a discount to make an immediate decision, we decided to take the information home and think it over.

On the drive home, I was filled with mixed emotions. I felt like I was never going to be able to reach my dream. Of course, now I realize that the entire process was a scam. Anyone who showed up for the evaluation was recruited. Their acceptance was not based on looks and talent, but rather on the ability to pay their tuition.

I was one of the fortunate ones. I didn't have enough money to attend the school, I lived too far away to commit to regular classes, and the school eventually stopped calling. If it was not for those simple facts, I could have just as easily been the main character of any of the stories listed below.

Scams are a serious problem in the entertainment business, and no one is immune. Remember, there ARE legitimate costs of doing business in this industry and one area is training. Not all schools are scams. For more information on how to tell if a school is a scam or not, please contact your local BBB.

All the stories below are true. Their names have been changed to protect the families' and their minor children's privacy.

Lost Dollars, Lost Dreams, Lost Hope: A Mother Ignores theTruth

A mother contacted me. I had judged her daughter in a pageant where she had placed in the top five. She had great potential, but she was just starting out. They wanted to know about my coaching and went on to tell me they were headed to Florida to attend a *special* modeling contest where "all the important people would be…"

I said to myself, "Red flag." I asked for some information, and I then proceeded to give her my opinion on what she may encounter at the Florida event. I explained what I thought she would gain (or wouldn't) versus what she really needed to be doing to get her daughter started in modeling, acting, or the pageant circuit.

This mother already knew that they had bought into the hype, but she could not get her money back. At this stage, she had talked herself into it beyond embarrassment and above the cost.

She wasn't expecting anything "really big" to happen for her daughter, but did not want to miss the opportunity "just in case." "How sad," I thought as I hung up the phone. Here is a mother who knows the truth and will not admit it and a daughter who will be strung along until it is too late. I also thought how perfect they had set themselves up for getting scammed. Not only did she let her pride get in the way of seeing the truth - once she finally learned it, she buried her head in the sand.

Another common phrase that is thrown around to entice parents to come to modeling contests, conventions, schools and pageants is, "You can make a family vacation out of it."

In situations like this, I tell the parents if they have disposable income and they choose to bring the family along for the trip: Just have fun. Do not get caught up in unnecessary spending and do not fall prey to false hopes.

What You Don't Know Can Cost You . . . A Ton of Money

"I grew up wanting to be a soap opera actress. Recently, I decided to pursue my dream. I went to a locally-owned modeling school "placement agency" and started their program. They stressed they are not an agency, but their classes were supposedly the key to getting in the business.

I was charged a ton of money for headshots and a couple of fairly useless classes. I wish I would've known before I got started I wasn't really going to get my money's worth. Now, I have to start over. Find some real classes, audition for student films and take extra roles in hopes of getting something on my résumé so I can get representation, a real agent."

"She was now officially invited to come to their 'academy' for proper lessons."

I heard a radio ad requesting models for an upcoming movie. I immediately told my daughter. This was right up her alley. She called the number and they scheduled her for a "cattle call" on that weekend.

Having done this before, we knew about cattle calls. One hundred kids showed up. They took everyone into a private room for an interview and discussed the application. They put each kid on a short video clip and dismissed them, telling us to call them the next day for the "results."

These people told us that of the hundreds of kids who interviewed, they narrowed it down to 20, and of course, they told me my daughter made the cut. She was now officially invited to come to their "academy" for proper lessons/training to the tune of $800 to $3500.

When they learned we couldn't come up with the money, suddenly her talents were of little use to them. We were escorted quickly to the door.

Don't Call Us. We'll Call YOU.

When our son was a year old, we signed him up at a mall for a local, well known modeling school/agency. They claimed to have work for babies. We paid money for the representation and got pictures taken for his composite cards.

Unfortunately for us, we had to get more pictures because the first batch was not "good enough." After almost $1000 and a year later, he still did not even get one audition. I called their offices on several occasions to find out when the auditions would be held. All they would say is they would call us.

When my son was two, we received a phone call from the agency. This call was a sales call to let us know they had an audition coming up for casting. We proceeded to take him into the agency. Once we got there, they began to run us through the process again. "We can get you work! We've represented the Olsen twins. You need a contract, you need pictures, sign here." After we let them go through their routine, we explained who we were. We told them that we already had a contract and that over the past year nobody has called us with any information.

Needless to say, their attitude towards us changed. "Oops! Your son must have fallen through the cracks with a previous employee of the agency. We can get you work now, but he will need new pictures since he is now another year older." After thinking about it for about five seconds, we asked for a refund and left immediately. Can you believe they contacted us by mail again six months later?

"I paid almost $1000 just for crappy pictures."

This "agency" promised me they would get me work. I first had to pay upfront money, $950, for a photo session with a "West Coast" photographer. I did.

> **Lar Says...**
> The ONLY legitimate reason an agent will ever ask you for money may be to print you in their agency "Headbook" or to cover your cost of being added to their web page. Agents are never paid until you have booked a job.

They printed out pictures for me, which looked horrible by the way, and then I never heard from them again. They never booked any work for me, but worst of all is that I paid almost $1000 just for crappy pictures.

It was a big mistake and it is almost as embarrassing to even say I fell for it. I was really young and did not know anything about the business. Watch out for any agency that is asking for money up front. It is amazing how many people do not know to look out for scams. I didn't!

"I let them make all the decisions. I trusted they knew what was best for her."

I had heard of this talent search often, so I decided to call for my daughter, Sarah. The cost would be approximately $1200 for her to perform a one-minute monologue in front of a panel of show business agents, personal managers, and casting directors.

What did we get for the $1200? We received the talent scout's industry connections, guidance, and the chance to have the industry professionals' attention for one minute.

I wrote the check, and the audition went great. She got one callback from a team of Hollywood personal managers. They said, "Get out here, get enrolled in school, get settled and explore the area." We were cautioned not to get involved much with other people because they are all here for the same reason and they will not have "your best interest at heart."

We moved to L.A. on the advice of these two and I placed my daughter's "career" completely in their hands. That was my mistake. I let them make all the decisions on when and who to contact about representing my daughter. I trusted they knew what was best for her. I never read a single book, talked to the Better Business Bureau, or even called the Screen Actors Guild.

Eventually I began researching and mailed out ten to fifteen headshots and résumés, and received a call from an agent within a week about a specific part in a soon-to-shoot pilot. I took my daughter to meet the agent. The following week, my daughter had an audition in front of the casting directors for this pilot. I had done in three weeks what the personal managers had failed to do in the preceding five months.

I found out what I should have been doing all along. Unfortunately, I figured this out too late. We had had enough.

Back home, Sarah happened to run into her managers. Later, I received a forwarded letter from them. It stated that they had done all they could for Sarah and that they were releasing her from her agreement. Even though they had seen us in the elevator back home, they hadn't even noticed we had left Los Angeles.

The Truth Finally Started to Come Out.

When I was in my twenties, I wanted to get into modeling and acting. There was modeling school and talent agency in my hometown, and it had a very good reputation. I had heard some of their graduates had gone on to New York and become successful.

I signed up with their talent agency. They sent me on a photo shoot and I took the basic and advanced courses, both of which cost me a lot of money.

When I called about jobs, the truth finally started to come out. I didn't really have the look they wanted to represent their agency. The school and agency knew all along that they would never place me in any real modeling job. They just wanted my money!

My advice to all these actors and models is to do their homework before shelling out any money for classes. Don't just talk to the school representatives; talk to other actors in the area. Find out from other industry professionals which schools are legitimate. You cannot trust the school's word alone. If their program is legitimate, you should be able to find working actors in your area who have benefited from it. If you cannot find one, run!

An Expert Says…

A $1,950.00 Tip

Jill Jaress, Actress, Filmmaker, Consultant
CEO Got a Laugh Entertainment
www.got-a-laugh.com
www.JillJaress.com

I was walking into a health food store on Ventura Boulevard in the San Fernando Valley, and saw a young woman walking out of an office with the word "Actors" on the door. I asked her what kind of business it was. She said happily, "Oh, it's fabulous! For only two thousand dollars, they pair you up with another actor, give you a scene and then have a showcase for everyone you need to know to get into show business. And they serve coffee and bagels at the showcase!"

I asked her what she meant by "everyone you need to know?" She said they were going to have a casting director, an agent, a producer and a director there to see their scenes. I asked her if she had already paid for the seminar. She said yes and they were going to have the performance in about an hour. I wished her the best of luck and went on my way.

It would not have done any good to tell her that there was a legitimate place right down the street, where she could have received the same results for fifty bucks --- sans the bagels.

The moral of this tale is NEVER, NEVER, NEVER pay this kind of money for a showcase of this type. It would be much better to just keep going on Equity and 99-seat-waiver auditions and land a part in a play. Then you can invite anyone everyone you want to see your work.

PART III

Where Do I Go From Here?

Too often, creative people think that their job ends at being creative. They neglect the other important part of the work – the *business*. So how does an actor market, manage expenses, invest, and take care of the books? Part III of this book is a crash course on the business side of performing.

CHAPTER 9

MARKETING MATERIALS AND LEGITIMATE EXPENSES

New headshots and postcards are invaluable tools – and great habits – that keep your name in the forefront of your agent's mind, and will also keep those auditions, readings, and callbacks coming.

What Do I Need and What Does It Cost?

You have a business and it is you. You are the product, the producer, the star, the casting office, the casting director and the writer. An office needs tools and you have chosen a low overhead business, which is good, but there are expenses. The prices will vary from area to area.

In effect, consider yourself a store that sells **YOU**. In order to get people interested in your product, you must believe in it. This means you have to be confident in your abilities. Then you must have advertising samples (headshots and résumés) that will attract customers to your store (a web presence and demo tapes). Because all business is competitive, you will also need to make sure your marketing materials are current.

> **Lar Says...**
> The number one complaint of casting directors is unprepared actors. You should always be proactive about gaining the knowledge which will put you in the best position to land the acting jobs you want. What does that mean? It means to learn the material, look up the director and producer. *Be prepared for your audition.*

Headshots

A professional headshot session will run about $300-$600. While you will not see many prices listed in this book for obvious reasons, headshot prices have remained standard for a number of years, defying normal market fluctuations. Some highly sought-after celebrity photographers will cost you more.

It's a wise idea to re-shoot your headshots twice a year, or as often as you can afford it. New hairdos, new roles, new wardrobe, new look - these are all great reasons to update your headshot.

Many times a fashion fad – be it on the rise or fading out – makes having a new headshot a must. Other times it's to capitalize on a series of roles you have recently portrayed. If you continue to be cast in a similar type of role or similar look, take that as a hint that you fit that type. Tailor your marketing materials to take advantage of what appears to be a natural fit for you.

Then again, sometimes your health or physical appearance dictates you update your headshot. For instance, if you've just had a baby and don't foresee yourself losing the baby weight for a few months, you don't want to misrepresent yourself in a size 6 if you're currently a size 10. Maybe you've had several callbacks for the academic type lately. You might want to get a headshot taken with glasses on, hair up, book in hand, etc. These are subtle differences, but they work. And when they do, it makes it well worth all that effort.

If you are inexperienced with photography or needing an update, hire a coach to style your shoot according to what you need. This ultimately *saves money*. With all the photos produced digitally, you can save money by not using a makeup artist, but you do need to know how to do it yourself. Hire a makeup artist for glamorous looks and for press photos.

Duplication
You need to duplicate your headshots at a printer. Start with the lowest

amount you can, usually 100-300 copies with your name and contact information.

Business Cards

You might think business cards are just for salespeople and producers, and you're right! But you *are* a salesperson. In this case, you're selling yourself as a product, along with your talents and your professionalism. You're also a producer. Through honing your craft, taking classes, going on auditions, and getting jobs, you will manage to "produce" a career for yourself. Therefore, you need a business card. You can find these in a variety of places, styles, and prices.

> **Lar Says...**
> Turn a business card into a mini résumé with photos and contact information. Use photo post cards to market your career and "announce" important information. Only your imagination determines how creative your materials can be.

(Order yours at TalentStart.net)

Photo Post Cards

These are used for thank you notes and announcements. Put your picture on one side and contact information on the other, and leave room for a short handwritten note and the receiver's address.

Place your vital – though not personal – contact information in a compact, easy-to-locate position. With the remaining space, consider adding some of these functional, fun, and useful features: These are easier than writing on an 8x10.

> **WARNING:**
> You've probably even seen them advertised for FREE on the internet, and under no circumstances should you fall for this ploy. There are very few areas where free pays off when it comes to our business; this is definitely NOT one of them! Instead, design a more personal version that best represents who you are as a professional.

1. Your picture
2. Your credits
3. Your agent's contact info/logo
4. Stats (height, hair, and eye color)
5. Web address
6. A performance review
7. A set picture (a photo of you on the set)

(Order Yours at TalentStart.net)

Comp Cards

If you are a model, you need a **Comp Card** that is two sided 8.5" x 5" with several photos and stats listed. For more information on comp (or Zed) cards, see Glossary of Terms.

Professional Résumé

A professionally-designed résumé is more than a listing of your professional credits typed out on a paper. You need a non-graphic résumé for your agent to post on their web site and you may want a more interesting résumé for you to take in on each audition. Much like your website or headshots, your résumé should be updated regularly. Keep a template handy on your computer at home that can be easily updated with new pictures, roles, classes, or whatever else you feel will best represent you.

Résumés are critical for auditions; you should never leave home without a few on hand. They're not as easy to carry as business cards, but they are just as vital and you never know when you'll be at the right place in the right time and need one.

As mentioned earlier, if you are not computer savvy, pay to have your résumés done professionally. It may seem like a dent in your budget at the time, but it will be well worth it in the long run.

Domain Name and E-mail Addresses

You need to own your own domain name such as www.larparklincoln.com. Your email address should be your name at your website, for example, lar@larparklincoln.com.

This is standard, simple, clean, and makes it easy to find you. Casting directors will not hunt you down. Be conscious of having difficult email address names and domains which are hard to remember. Do not use free services, as it only looks as professional as it costs. Purchase your own domain name **today.**

Let me remind you at this point the importance of email signatures. Sending an email without a signature is similar to sending a letter without a signature. Common courtesy and business sense dictate signing your emails with additional contact information below your name.

Web Site

Just as it is important to have a business card to hand out physically, it's also important to have a space reserved in cyberspace. Business is done on the web, including casting, scouting, and researching.

A website and email address are as cutting edge as the phone originally was. Having a website to capitalize on this modern practice is good business and just plain common sense. You can spend hundreds, even thousands on websites, but you don't have to do that.

When building a web site, work with your designer to keep it simple. Avoid using complicated features that will end up costing you more money and will not reap any benefits in return. You need a basic one- to five-page site that can accommodate a downloadable résumé and demo. Include your name and contact information on every page.

You can have a list of credits on one page (résumé), assorted poses/styles of alternate headshots and/or body shots on another, a biography page on another, testimonials from producers, directors, colleagues, etc., on another.

An actor's websites should feature a demo of his or her work, which can be played with just the click of a mouse. You should also have a slate on your website.

Make it attractive, informative, and at all times, user-friendly. If a casting director must try too hard to locate your contact information, they will move on to someone easier to find.

A basic four-page site contains the following: a home page, various headshots, a résumé/biography, and a voice or demo. Here are some ideas for optional pages that might set you apart from the pack:

1. An Appearing Soon page with upcoming roles
2. A Character page with headshots shots or pictures "in character," from the set on which you have worked

3. A guestbook – helps you keep track of people on your "team" to send email updates
4. A links page to other actors' sites or useful information

Acting Demo
Demos are a specialized field and they need to be short and showcase you. Even if you do not have any student, independent, or professional scenes to edit onto a reel, you still need to be able to demonstrate your ability. Most agents require a demo prior to setting up an initial interview. Limit demos to less than two minutes.

Your greatest time and money investment comes from gathering the work. Although you will still need continual updates, it will never be as difficult as the first time. *Keep all masters in the original digital format.*

Collect the performances that you wish to put on your reel, *which is not easy.* Try to get it as soon as possible after shooting. Production offices often close up shop after a show is finished and getting your copy can be a nightmare.

Much like you update your résumé and headshot as often as possible, your demo should be an evolving creature that grows and expands along with your range of experiences. Think of the demo as a living résumé or headshot: it's there to represent you when you can't be there to represent yourself.

If your experience is limited to commercials, films, extra work, or live theater, these can be recorded and presented on your demo. Accordingly, make sure your demo is of the best quality possible. This is another one of those areas where you shouldn't scrimp. If you can't afford to have a demo reel professionally produced, be innovative. When I couldn't afford to have my headshots professionally photographed early in my career, I volunteered at a photography studio in exchange for headshots. Whenever I heard the words "test shoot," or TFP (trade for print) when a photographer is sampling a new background, lens, or form of lighting, I jumped at the chance and volunteered continuously until I had a good free headshot. You can do the same by volunteering at studios – they always need people to do clerical or office work. Do this in exchange for producing a demo reel *you* can be proud of.

Voice Demo

A voice demo CD can be extremely valuable. Voice work pays well and is fun. You will probably spend $800 to $1200 for a high quality voice demo that you can use to market your own voice. This fee involves voice taping and tailoring the copy to your voice. Usually several copies are included. These demos will be put on your website also. You will need to update as you progress. If you are interested in voice over work, upload a voice demo to your website. Of course, the more experience you have, the more your demo will grow. Like your demo, keep voice demos under two minutes. Preferably voice demos would be 30-second, 60-second, and 90-second only.

Press Kit

What makes up a press kit? As the name implies, this is a "kit" that involves any "press" you may have received, such as good reviews, newspaper clippings, kudos from fellow actors or industry professionals. These should appear in a professional-looking format including headshots, your résumé/professional biography, and perhaps a demo. Today, your press kit can also be "electronic." Materials should be kept in one folder, ready to e-mail.

Digital Camera

Have a digital camera handy for submitting current digital shots. You also need it to have with you on the set to collect shots of you working, so you can add these *on set photos* to your websites, reproduce for thank you cards, as well as design your photo post cards and stationery.

Training

There are some professions that allow you to earn your credentials, and that completes your professional education. *Not showbiz.* It would just be ludicrous for an actor to think he or she could take this same approach. You cannot study for "X" amount of time and then be done with it. The industry is always changing, and you have to plan and budget for continued learning and training; otherwise, your career will become stagnant.

Consider classes in cold reading, scene study, voice, movement, film technique, on-camera technique, monologues, improvisation, commercial training, ear prompter, teleprompter, and auditioning skills. An actor's training should involve your face, voice, and body. Keep all of your actor's tools sharp and conditioned.

Window Envelopes

Window envelopes are vital when submitting your headshot and résumé. The purpose for window envelopes is to make it easier for casting offices to quckly separate you into the correct "character piles" before ever having to open an envelope. Remember these offices get hundreds (if not thousands) of submissions daily. They will appreciate your extra effort.

Mobile Office Supplies

Always have a stapler and highlighter, access to a copy machine, computer, fax machine, cell phone, and car (unless you live in New York and can take the train).

Savings

Plan on having six months of living expenses before moving away from your home and family to pursue your career. Read Judy Kerr's book <u>Acting Is Everything: An Actor's Guidebook for a Successful Career in Los Angeles</u>. Even though it says "Los Angeles" in the title, the research applies in all major film markets. In short, add all costs, including hair, clothes, food, and so on, then double it.

> **Lar Says...**
> Whatever you print, someone will disapprove. The next teacher you study with will have a different opinion. The rules will vary, *and the rules will stay the same.* The actor bragging about all the work he is doing probably isn't. Most likely he does not have *any* work. Use your common sense. Keep grounded, stick to your plan, and work your plan.

Information Overload

Much of this information can feel overwhelming, especially at first. Create your own *Timeline to Stardom™ Checklist* and break the overwhelming projects into manageable tasks. You will find that each step builds upon the other. Before you know it, your career is underway.

Industry Immersion

One key to succeeding in this industry is immersion. You need to completely immerse yourself. In order to succeed, you have to live it, love it, breathe it, eat it and sleep it. You have to embrace this career in all aspects.

Read about your craft. Not just acting and monologue books but also business books like this one. Learn how to manage your money. Read the trade papers to see who is doing what. Go to the Internet Movie Database

(IMDB.com). Spot the trends and learn what is going on and where it is happening.

Watch as many entertainment shows as you can, and be in the know as to what is going on. Becoming knowledgeable about any industry is what successful people do. Continue to arm yourself with information, inspiration, and a determination to succeed.

Knowledge is power, and in this business, you'll need all the power you can get. Knowledge helps you *feel* powerful and confident. When you are confident, it shows.

> What is most important in pursuing your craft is how to be a good business person. Learn how to start and operate your business, sell your product, make a profit and you will stay in business.
>   Bob Fraser, YouMustAct.com

A Lost Opportunity

If you're not prepared, you will not succeed. For example, even though I am not a casting director, I occasionally get calls for my students. A job came in for a commercial featuring two teenagers talking on the telephone – for non-union actors – and it was going to pay a generous salary plus cover the agency fee. The part required a Hispanic girl between the ages of 12 and 14. I had a few students that were absolutely perfect for the role.

I got this notice at 9 pm on a Monday night, and I immediately contacted the actor.

The parents' response went something like this:

> "This seems like such short notice. We have not duplicated her résumés and pictures yet, so we don't know if we can make the audition on time."

Long story short: They didn't go.

I got a note the next day from the casting director. She said she had so many fabulous actors come to the audition that not only was she able to cast that commercial immediately, but also cast several other projects representing the Hispanic market. This is a good example of how quickly things can happen in this industry when *opportunity* meets *preparation*. Performers can book several jobs at once. Unfortunately, the student I was so excited to send over was not prepared and lost the opportunity of a lifetime.

CHAPTER 10

TIMELINE TO STARDOM™

The Master List

What's a master list, you ask? Well, as one might guess, this is a list of people you already know. You may have worked with them (cast, crew), submitted to them (casting directors, productions), mingled with them at industry functions (coaches, writers, publicists). These are people who you would like to keep in touch with throughout the course of your career.

How do you create a master list of your own? Take a minute and remember about the people you have worked with. Has anyone ever complimented you on work you have done? Have you received notes from others saying they enjoyed working with you or thought you did a particular scene well? Of course you have. *Or you will soon.*

> **Lar Says...**
> A master list once solidified, and updated regularly can become your personal plan for stardom.

Now start writing down the names with a brief note next to each – you can go into more detail later. For now you are simply trying to jog your memory. This isn't a novel you're writing here; just a quick note to remind you of how that person has impacted you and any contact information you might need to get in touch with them.

Start your Master List here by naming your first 25 contacts.

1. _____
2. _____
3. _____
4. _____
5. _____
6. _____
7. _____
8. _____
9. _____
10. _____
11. _____
12. _____
13. _____
14. _____
15. _____
16. _____
17. _____
18. _____
19. _____
20. _____
21. _____
22. _____
23. _____
24. _____
25. _____

No matter how successful you are, taking the best advice can be daunting, even when it's your own. Case in point: I was watching a movie and when I saw the credits, I realized I had worked with the director before several years earlier. The show was great! I was proud of him and his accomplishment, but at the same time I realized I hadn't heeded my own advice about contacting my "master list" as hard and heavy as I should have been.

We have all heard the expression "it's who you know." I have always felt that phrase had a negative sound to it – as if we didn't work for what we earned; that "someone" knew "someone" who gave us the job; or that we "used" or tried to use someone to get where we are. Any of which might be true, but it doesn't have to be. If you create a win-win situation for everyone, you aren't "using" people. Unless we are connected by family to the biz, we all start out *"not knowing"* anyone. I didn't know a soul in the industry. I prefer to turn the phrase around from a negative to a positive, as in, "Yes, it is who you know and who you will get to know and who you keep in touch with and who they know that they can refer you to…" As long as you are genuine with those you meet and with whom you network, you aren't taking advantage of them. Instead, you both mutually benefit by sharing successes.

As you develop your master list, you may be overcome with both excitement and even sadness. Why excitement AND sadness? Sadness can occur because you may have realized that you should have taken some time and jotted off a few "thinking of you" notes. The excitement is because you will soon realize that you have a built-in fan club and you didn't even know you were already a star!

I know it can seem difficult to get started on this overwhelming task. Here is an easy tip to help you begin "remembering" all of the people that need to be on your list: look back over your day planner, appointments, auditions, interviews, etc. From there, move on to your stacks of holiday cards from the last few years, letters and notes, your email address book, and before you know it, your master list will start to mushroom into something uncontrollable. Now *that's* a good problem to have!

The next step – and of course you must realize that this list will continue to grow – is to set up your master list in a database on a computer. You might be wondering, "How does this list help you start, maintain and grow your career?" Here is an analogy: You can be the best actor on the planet.

At the same time, if you end up on the cutting room floor because you lacked technical skills, no one will know how terrific you are except the walls. Think of this as a tool. You have to be sure that the people in the industry know what is happening in your business. In other words, you need to advertise. The best place to start is with your master list!

Free Publicity
Early in your career, you won't be able to hire a press agent, so become your *own* publicist. Acquire the names of all local newspapers, local radio, television, and cable shows. Start where you live and add the cities where you were born, raised, graduated, are attending school or church. Send anyone and everyone a press release with the details of your performances or accomplishments.

Newspapers and local magazines need new stories every day. It's not easy but you may soon find yourself getting a mention or even an entire article.

Developing a strong relationship with your Agent
Many actors complain how their agent "doesn't do anything" for them… Yes they do! Agents work very hard for many clients. Remember you are not their only client. So much of their work is intangible and consists of actions that you never see. Many agents have complained about how "these actors are so flakey – why can't they get it together?" Actors work very hard, too. The problem is most actors have not learned how to manage their careers.

I would like to share a story with you a story from agent and friend, Nancy Johnson. While visiting Nancy's office, a beautiful actress came in. She positively lit up the room. Her face glowed, her hair was perfect, she had a great figure, and her smile was infectious.

She and Nancy went over some auditions and business, and then she left. Afterwards, I commented to Nancy on how striking I thought she was. Apparently she was multi-talented also: Nancy bragged about her many talents – a triple threat. She could sing, dance and act. I personally have to "act" like I can do either of the other two skills!

"Why didn't this actress get more work?" I inquired. Being in marketing, I asked to see her headshots. Nancy replied that the actress's headshots were on the wall in the very room in which we were sitting. I looked and, not finding a picture that looked even remotely like the stunning star I had just met asked again, "Nancy, where?"

When I saw the headshot, I knew the answer: the actress hadn't updated her materials in a long time. It was not the look she sported today. She just wasn't "minding her store," so to speak. Nancy shrugged her shoulders and sighed as she asked rhetorically: "How can I want it more than they do?"

I knew what she meant: many more opportunities could come along for that actress *if* she wanted them to or if she understood marketing. How many times does a talent have to be told to update their materials and be sure the agent has a supply in the office for distribution? It's your career, your business, and you are the executive producer. Take charge, take control, and then bask in the limelight that you will have earned.

What an Actor Earns

Union actors (actors in the Screen Actors Guild) must be paid a certain amount of money depending on the role. For example, an actor may be paid $800 for one day's work shooting a commercial. Wow! That sounds like an incredible salary, and it would be if you earned it regularly, but acting doesn't work that way. Jobs are few and far in between. Remember, actors have spent years taking classes, paying for pictures, and all of the marketing materials we have discussed. Until you reach star status and have an agent who can negotiate higher day rates, that day's earnings (along with your day jobs) may have to carry you for several months.

If we break down the costs of what is taken out of this actor's check, we'll discover what *really* ends up in the bank.

He shoots the commercial and receives $800. Right off the top of that figure, he must pay his agent 10% or $80. Now it's time to pay his manager, who can take anywhere from 10 to 20% of his earnings. Let's assume he has a manager who takes 15% or $120. You now have a balance of $600 from your original $800.

Oh, but wait a minute. You've got taxes on that $800. If you are in 15% tax bracket, you owe 15% of your earnings to taxes, which is another $120. Depending on where you live, you may also have state tax of 8% or

$64, as well. Of course taxes are going to be offset, particularly in the beginning, by your legitimate tax deductions.

That makes 80 bucks for your agent, 120 dollars for your manager, and now another 184 bucks for taxes! Do you see how the 800 dollars starts to dwindle? That leaves you $416, but that's not all free and clear profit. Take into consideration the time spent auditioning, the time you lost when you had to take off work from your day job to both audition and shoot the commercial, fuel for the audition and shoot, and so on.

> **Lar Says...**
> Ask any star and they will say, "I'm paid for the hassle, I act for free!"

Is there an upside to this equation? Yes. Being a union actor entitles you to benefits and residuals. Every time that commercial is played, you will receive a residual check in the mail. If it is a national commercial (one that runs country wide), it can easily add $25,000 to $100,000 to your bank account yearly. While there are many national commercials, there are also many local and regional commercials that do not pay out large residuals. In other words, you cannot count on the idea of large checks coming on a regular basis.

According to the Bureau of Labor Statistics, the median earnings for actors was only $23,462 in 2005, with the middle 50 percent earning between $16,000 and $64,000 annually. Movie and television actors and actresses tend to earn more than stage performers. Pay is usually based on the number of performances given, except for movie actors who generally receive a lump sum and possibly a portion of the royalties for each film. Many actors belong to Equity, the Screen Actors Guild, or other unions whose collective bargaining agreements set minimum salaries, hours of work, and other conditions of employment for acting parts.

> This is a good time to evaluate your love of this career. Are you willing to be an informed, smart talent who can plan, budget, and prepare for your future (i.e. follow the steps outlined in this book)? Or are you simply dreaming of celebrity and star status, while unwilling to put forth the effort? The celebrities you see on TV make it look effortless because that is their job. Every successful actor has a story of tenacity, determination, ingenuity, and perseverance leading up to the point where you recognize his or her face.

An Expert Says…

To Stand Out – You Have to be Outstanding!

Mary Ann Halpin, Photographer
Goddess of the Camera
Muse of Creativity
www.MaryAnnHalpin.com

Pictures are the most important marketing tools for an actor You should partner with your photographer to create . . . a powerful image . . . an image that will make a casting director pause to really look at it. We want that casting director to put that photo into the "yes" file and not "file 13", the trash.

The eyes are the windows of the soul.

When you look at a headshot , put your hands over the entire picture and just reveal the eyes. What are those eyes saying to you? Do they convey confidence, happiness and joy? Or do they look fearful and uncomfortable?   Make sure when you are having your photos taken that you feel as comfortable as possible, because the camera doesn't lie. I believe that people really react to the energy and emotion of a photograph rather than the photo itself. Your confidence level and a real connection to the camera are important and must come from a real place inside of you. If you force an expression or feel phony it will look phony. When you are having fun, feeling relaxed, you will look that way in your photo.

I have photographed actors for over two decades. Some of these actors have become very successful. A few years ago, I photographed a beautiful young actress, Constance Zimmer. I started photographing her when she was 19 years old. She had the "It" factor. She was cute, funny and smart. There are many girls in Los Angeles that have those qualities but Constance was just a little different. She knew her strengths and she played to them. She was a cute character and she promoted herself as that.

She had a signature look with a blunt cut hairstyle with bangs. She created an image that would garner the parts that reflected that image .When every other actress in town started copying her look, she decided to change it and grow out her bangs. So we did a photo session for her new look. It may sound simple but it is very important to pay attention to the trends and also creating a trend.

She was soon cast in several shows in a recurring role; Good Morning Miami, Joan of Arcadia, Entourage and most recently Boston Legal. She is cast in very interesting, slightly quirky parts. Constance continues to have an outstanding career as a working actress.

Some people think you are born with the "It" factor. I am not so sure. I have seen many actors create a great career because they are smart about putting their image together and know how to market themselves. I have seen incredibly talented actors who never make it because they don't have the drive and stamina to do what is necessary to be successful.

I see headshot portraiture as an emotional dance creating a magical synergy between the actor and the camera.

Enjoy your dance!

Brooke   Isabella

CHAPTER 11

ON-SET ETIQUETTE

I learned very early that not responding to an invitation or failing to follow directions would cause me great pain and frustration later in life.

One of the department stores in our area would run a fashion model search every year. Fortunately for me, it wasn't a scam. It was a legitimate teen fashion group. This kind of work can sometimes still be found in local malls. Department Stores or boutiques compile a group of teens from local schools and develop a fashion advisory board that does fashion shows to promote their store and other mall events.

The teen board I was on would get together for fashion luncheons several times during the year. Each girl received a beautiful invitation to the Spring Show including when and where to get all of the information to audition and begin rehearsals; but first we needed to attend an orientation and luncheon. As you might have already guessed, I was really excited.

There were 4 little letters at the bottom of the page: RSVP. These are the same letters you will still see at the bottom of invitations today; hopefully you do not neglect them.

RSVP is the abbreviation of the French phrase *Respondez, s'il vous plait.* Its literal translation is: Respond, please. It means to let the host or hostess know if you will be attending. This is important, because people hosting functions, parties, and events must have an idea of the number of people attending so they can plan the food, the goodie bags, the hors d'oeuvres, the seating arrangements, and anything else they might need for the event to be a success.

Lar Says...
You need to develop a system designed to file your invitations and keep track of all your appointments and auditions. You don't want to miss important dates and times, and you don't want to go through the humiliation and embarrassment that can come from forgetting to RSVP.

I saw those words on the invitation, and I knew I was supposed to RSVP, but I procrastinated. I would pay the consequences for that hesitation later.

The day came, and I dressed for success. My mother scheduled her day to drive me. I gathered my invitation and jumped in the car and off we went to the regular meeting place.

As I walked up to the room, I noticed there was a sign on the door. Signs on doors are generally not good things when you are arriving for parties or events. I saw a few other teen fashion board models standing around looking frustrated. I soon knew why.

The sign read: "Would love to have you join our party and be in the biggest fashion show of the year. Apparently, you didn't RSVP to get the proper directions to the location where we'll be meeting. Have a great day. Good luck next year getting on the panel."

There was no way to find out where the event was being held, either in the store or in the mall. I did not get to do the fashion show in the spring, and I failed to make the board the next year. It was a very silent ride home.

Some might say that was a little harsh for 14-year-old girl, but I believe it was right on target. I think by the time you are a teen, you should have manners and social graces so that you don't become the victim of your own procrastination.

I understood that day that if I failed to RSVP on anything then I was *failing to make a decision, and a decision would be made for me.* I learned I didn't like that very well, and I was both disappointed and embarrassed. The lesson I took away from that experience was that making no decision *is* a decision.

This was early in my career. Since that time, I have painstakingly checked and double checked call sheets, locations, and all other requirements. While I made sure never to make a mistake like that again, I have been in a position to observe others derail their own careers – or at least suffer serious setbacks – which could have easily been avoided.

The High Cost of Oversleeping

Unless the earth is moving, which it has been known to do in Los Angeles, I am not late. Being late is rude to other people and is disrespectful of them. When you're late to a go-see or an audition, you put your agent in a bad position, because they made the appointment for you. You also put yourself in a bad light because you're unprepared. Casting is not happy, because they have to juggle the schedule around you. The other people waiting for appointments with the Casting Director are affected because now they, too, must all wait on you.

I worked on a TV series for ABC as a guest star. We started early in the morning and went late into the day. The ongoing series was full of veteran TV actors. After arranging for double alarms and a "just in case" back up phone call, I got plenty of sleep so I was on time for my set call. I worked too hard for too many years to be *late*!

The actress who was in the first shot didn't show. After about 15 minutes, production decided to skip her scene and jumped to mine instead. I had finished make-up and wardrobe, and was very well prepared so the last minute change didn't concern me as far as my own performance. Production continued to try to locate their missing actress. A ripple effect began. The lighting crew had to move everything and everyone had to change gears to set up in a new location for a different scene.

Being a guest star, I was booked only a couple of days out of the week to do my part. The other actress was critical to my role, however, because she was playing a villain and to complete my scenes, we needed her.

When she finally did show up, she ran into the makeup room huffing and puffing and in tears. "I can't believe this. I can't believe this is happening. I literally overslept. I just overslept. What should I tell them?"

We all work too hard to get a job just to oversleep once it's ours. Perhaps she was anxious and excited about her role and couldn't sleep. When she finally did sleep, it was deep. In a city like Los Angeles, missing the smallest time slot on the freeway equals being late.

She was supposed to be the first shot of that day. She was told every couple of hours that she would be up next, but who do you think was shooting the last shot of that day as we went overtime at 10 o'clock that night? It was her scene. They had moved her all the way from the first scene of the day to the last scene of the day. Who knows how it affected her performance? I'm pretty sure she learned an important lesson. Have a back-up alarm clock and be on time!

When you are late to work at a job where there are 3 or 4 people depending on you, say in an office or a restaurant, you inconvenience a handful of people. In some businesses, there is usually a degree of flexibility.

Showbiz is different. When you work on a film or a modeling shoot, you are the one and only person for the job. A great deal of difficulty took place to cast the perfect person. For instance, wardrobe designed the outfit(s) for you; a PR or advertising company wrote the script or developed the ad; the list goes on and on. Casting, contracts, etc. have all taken place. Everything depends on your punctuality: the lighting, the sets, the very expensive rental equipment, and the other actors or models in the scene with you. Can you see how easy it might be to mess up an entire day's schedule – and even the next day's schedule – and cost the production company or the advertising agency a lot of money and time because you were just "a few minutes late?" To add to the embarrassment, they call your agent, they call your manger, they call your home, they call your car, they call your dog, and with each message it becomes more and more clear that when you finally get there, the entire cast and crew is *not* going to be happy with you!

Being late when you are an employee is very rude to your boss and the company you work with. It is form of stealing. Goods are priced depending on how much they cost to produce and make. You are a product and you are supposed to be on the set on time so they can get it in the can (which means wrap it up) and get it to the editor on time. He will edit it and then get it back to producers and directors and the network so that it can be approved and get it out on the airwaves so everyone can see it. Many people's schedules are riding on your alarm clock.

The night before a job is not the night to go out and party. In fact, excessive partying will only hurt your career. You may have a lot of fun in the beginning with it, but eventually, inevitably, it will start to take its toll. Late nights, poor health care, and neglecting personal grooming will start to show up on your face, your attitude, and everything else about you. People who party all night, every night, are not reliable. Drugs and alcohol may be in every business in the world, but they don't belong in this business anymore than they belong in any other.

A Few Words on How to Avoid Being Late

To avoid being late like my co-star was, take a minute when you get a job, or an audition, to map out how long it's going to take to get you there. If you can, you should make a "practice drive" to the studio the night before. Other things you can do to prepare and avoid being late include packing what you will need in the car before you go to sleep and charging the cell phone so it's ready to go in the morning.

Start practicing now. Show self-respect and respect for others by being on time to school, work, and all acting and modeling related events. Become the punctual performer directors will trust. Make it your business to develop an image of professionalism that will stay with you.

Thank goodness we have websites and GPS devices that can get you to your destination very easily. If you are in one of the larger cities, you will find that you often have more than one audition and/or appointment on the same day. You might also be dropping off headshots at one location, picking up wardrobe somewhere else, planning a photo session at yet another place, attending a class, and getting a call back.

If you will be going to multiple appointments in a day, plan in advance by neatly packing all of the clothes for each appointment. Pack food, because you are not always going to have time to grab something healthy to eat. Not only will you eat healthier, you may save money when you need it most.

Be sure you have all of your scripts and your directions from one appointment to the next in order throughout the day. Take into consideration possible callbacks that will inevitably spring up right in the middle of your busy day. Map all of this out the night before, yet be prepared and flexible for the unexpected.

Take acting books with you. If you are in school, of course, use the time between appointments to study and complete your homework. If you are out of school, take something to occupy your time.

Make Mondays through Fridays your work days. Plan your day around your auditions and your interviews as though they are your job.

Some people need very organized days – they function better with a specific schedule. That's probably not the easiest personality to have if you are planning to be in this business. You are required to be flexible because of the "Controlled Chaos."

A Few Words about Being on the Set

Early in your career, you may find the set can feel uncomfortable. It isn't like a supportive acting class. It's noisy. Everyone seems to be running around in a thousand different directions. Someone's handing you **script revisions**, which are new lines you need to learn right away. Hair and makeup people are attending to you, producers are having meetings, the **craft service** people are preparing meals for large numbers of cast and crew, **transportation** are the Teamsters who move heavy equipment, the **best boys** are moving lights and camera equipment . . . all of this activity is happening while you are trying to get ready emotionally and physically to do a scene.

It can seem overwhelming. You may feel you don't know how you can possibly concentrate or focus on anything. But here's the good news: you do have what it takes. You got the part!

There are specific words and phrases used in our industry that you simply won't hear anywhere else. Familiarize yourself and your child ahead of time with the terms. If you have a young child, you might want to teach the phrases and quiz him or her later. This way, the child feels more comfortable and is more knowledgeable on the set.

You are going to hear new vocabulary. These may not even be words. Rather, these important sounds help guide (and are very meaningful to) the mass of people working. You may hear a **buzzer** or a **bell** sound; this is called (on a bell). It means the crew is filming and you must be extremely quiet. Make sure you're absolutely frozen; don't even walk when you are on a bell. All noise can be captured, causing costly retakes if directions are not followed. When you hear a **double bell** or a **couple of short rings** (off a bell), you know you can resume talking quietly or moving around.

At the entrance to the set, if you see a **flashing** or **solid red light**, that's a warning that the crew is filming – DO NOT ENTER OR EXIT! Trust me, you don't want to open those heavy doors and make a noise in the middle of someone's scene. (This is NOT the kind of entrance you are hoping to make!)

Another word you may hear is **speed**, which means to get the camera rolling. Then you'll hear **rolling**, which cues the director, cinematographer and crew that the cameras are rolling, followed by **action**. You may hear "action" for background actors to begin their movements prior to your cue.

One of the most important words you are going to hear is **cut**. It means the camera has been instructed to stop filming and the scene is over and/or needs to be redone. Don't worry when this happens: Usually scenes need to be re-shot for technical reasons. Actors do not ever, under any circumstances, "cut" a scene! If you have done something to cause the director to say "cut," you will be told what to do differently. And you should not break character immediately. The cameras are slow to stop rolling, so stay in character. At the end of a long day, you will be happy to hear, "**It's a wrap**." It signals the end of shooting for the day.

Lights, Camera, Action!

An Expert Says…

Acting for the Camera

Tony Barr, Author & Film Coach
www.FilmActorsWorkshop.com

Teachers must be aware of a time factor as they train actors for the film and television industry. Someone decides to become an actor and enrolls in a workshop. In a few months that actor goes out to find an agent and to meet casting people and soon that young and inexperienced actor is getting roles.

The reason for his quick success is that in the film and television media an actor's quality is often more important than his talent level.

The intimate nature of the camera is largely responsible for that standard. It is not important that the actor move well, have a well trained voice, or be able to play an in-depth characterization from O'Neil or Miller or Shakespeare; it is primarily important that he have the quality the director wants for a particular role. It therefore becomes our responsibility (as coaches) to help the actor develop that quality and to free him so that he can give his natural talent its fullest expression. In this way, he will be as ready as possible to handle a role when his special quality wins it for him. That is why I approach training as I do and why I use camera equipment from the very beginning to train students.

The truth is that countless students find themselves working professionally in a very short time. They may not get starring roles, they may not get many lesser roles, but they do get work. It is very unlikely that they're going to be asked to improvise or do an exercise in concentration or sense memory; therefore I feel that the best and most important preparation for them is work with scenes so that they will be prepared for what they have to do when they get that first call.

Intuition. It is a long held theory that talent can be destroyed by studying acting and that an actor should depend on his intuition. The common statements are "Either you got it, or you ain't" and "Actors are born, not made" intuition is a lovely thing to have on your side. It is also a very treacherous thing, because sooner or later you are going to turn to it to help and it is not going to be around. At that point, you better have some know-how and some craft available to help you get through the rough spots facing you – to help you find your performance when intuition has failed.

> A question I am always asked is "What do you think about going to New York or Hollywood?" My answer is always the same; if you want to work in the theater, go to New York. If you want to work in film or television, go to Hollywood. If you can live without it, don't go to either one. If you *can't* live without it, don't let anybody stop you…

I genuinely believe that if you have the stamina and the determination to become and actor and if you can take the disappointments that will probably be your lot, you will eventually make your living as an actor, even though you may not become a star. You must, however, have the determination and you must work, work, work and continue to work to perfect your craft – to free and develop your instrument so that when an opportunity comes, you will be ready for it.

Ultimately the audience and only the audience can determine who is a star. No matter how talented you are your peers in the industry think you are, if the audience does not take to you, stardom is not your fate.

CHAPTER 12

SUCCESS SIGNS AND FOLLOWING UP

How Do **You** Define Success?

Success comes in many different forms, and is unique to every person. Sometimes success comes in signs, big signs, movie poster signs, billboard signs, fabulous magazine layouts, and awards. Sometimes success comes in smaller ways. You have to determine what YOUR success signs are. To solely equate money to success is to miss so many wonderful opportunities. If your goal is to make huge amounts of money and become famous, re-examine your objectives. Earning lots of money will most likely be the result of years of work and sacrifices. Passing celebrity is often purchased by putting a high-priced public relations firm on your payroll.

I want to inspire you to feel successful, no matter where you currently are in your career.

Some days I consider it a success if I just actually can get up and get everyone where they need to go, the kids to school, the dogs fed, and maybe my hair washed before noon. As both a full-time actor and mother, I often work late into the nights, overnights on shoots, and then again during the day.

If you are a person who needs very organized days – structured hours and unwavering schedules - this is probably not the business for you. You will not feel success, you will feel frustration. Only you can determine this for yourself. Performers are required to be flexible because of the "Controlled Chaos" I've mentioned before. Maybe you were scammed once, and now, after reading this book, you know not to ever get taken by a scam artist again. That is a successful feeling! Maybe you've pulled together a great résumé, a website, and a bio that makes people say "Wow." That's a success.

Perhaps for you, signing with your first agent is a real success story. I know it was for me. Success could be the first time you get a booking. Or the first time you work as an extra. Maybe it's the first time you get a check in the mail. Or you simply stumble into a career you love that's not in front of the camera, but *behind* the camera. You never know how roadblocks might turn into detours. I hid my first pregnancy during *Knots Landing*, and even won a *Soap Opera Digest* award for "best hidden pregnancy". While pregnant, I was introduced to voiceover work through my friend and actress Donna Mills. I loved it! I still do today. Perhaps an unexpected detour will also bring *you* unexpected rewards and introduce you to a career you never dreamed you would enjoy

Here are a few ideas that may help you to feel successful. You will add to this list as you grow as a person and an artist. Have fun checking off each success as you attain it.

Thirty Success Signs
- ☐ Feel stronger about yourself and your self-esteem.
- ☐ Learn and master a skill.
- ☐ Don't get taken by a scam again.
- ☐ Get a great headshot… It is yours forever.
- ☐ Put together a terrific résumé.
- ☐ Sign with an agent.
- ☐ Get a callback.
- ☐ Book a part.
- ☐ Work as an extra.
- ☐ Learn on the film set.
- ☐ Feel the pride of knowing you have sustained consistently focused auditions over a period of time.
- ☐ Declare yourself as an actor on your tax return for the very first time.
- ☐ Join the union.
- ☐ Cash your first residual check (be sure and copy it first for memories!).
- ☐ See your name on screen for the first time.
- ☐ See your*self* on screen for the first time.
- ☐ Start thinking in terms of "I am" instead of "I wish I were."
- ☐ Follow-up automatically.
- ☐ Remember to get pictures of yourself on the set.
- ☐ Remember to get pictures at an industry function.
- ☐ Get on the IMDB (Internet Movie Database).

□ Gather quotes and reviews and suddenly discover the process is actually painless.
□ Get nominated and/or win an industry award.
□ Work on a project that is being submitted for a film festival.
□ Write your own one-person show, comedy act, film, or short pilot.
□ Start an actors' network and action group.
□ A beginning actor asks for *your* advice.
□ People call from your home town to say they saw your work.
□ Someone asks for your autograph (and it's NOT on a check!).
□ You walk your *first* red carpet.

Think about your measures of success and celebrate each little victory along the way. Do not worry about the downtime – as they say, this too shall pass.

Fame, Family, and Friends

What do friends and family think about your business? From my perspective, what they think, feel, and say can vary greatly from person to person. When you choose a creative field or any field that's more public than other careers, your support system (i.e. your family and friends) can become very opinionated. Generally, there are two reactions. The first reaction might be something like, "Wow, that's so cool!" followed quickly by the second reaction which sounds something like this: "What's the matter with you? Are you crazy?" I've had them both.

Let's examine these reactions and see what they really mean. If you get the "Wow" reaction, it can mean you've been an outgoing person in your family, you've performed in dance and school theatre performances. Your family is comfortable with you being onstage, and they may have even encouraged you to go into the field. This type of supportive reaction comes from those who believe in you, and they are excited for you when you go into the business.

You may need to move to New York or Los Angeles. You may need to borrow seed money from your family to help pay your living expenses. If you do borrow money, no matter what, pay it back! Protect your integrity. Count on getting a job or two or three to help support yourself. It is okay if you need to save up additional seed money to give your business a more solid foundation and some capital to have a financial cushion.

I highly recommend three terrific advisors who specialize in finances: Dave Ramsey (www.daveramsey.com), who will teach you exactly how to manage your finances and live with respect; Suze Orman (www.suzeorman.com), a financial planner who will also teach you to live within a budget and keep whatever money you earn; and Mary Hunt (www.debtproofliving.com), also a terrific site for budgeting and planning.

The second reaction can come from genuinely concerned family, neighbors, and friends who don't want you to get hurt or scammed. They don't know anything about the business. They don't know that getting a role can take hundreds of auditions, nor do they realize that it is a business and you can earn a pension and a health plan and make a good living without ever becoming a recognized "star." People who aren't in the biz might say things such as, "I have an uncle or a cousin or a brother who is in New York or Los Angeles 'trying' to be an actor or a model. He's done a few small parts, but never *made it*. He spends so much time working odd jobs, and it's so expensive and he never seems to get anywhere. I wonder when he's going to give it up." These people don't understand the years it can take for someone to establish this type of career!

This career isn't guaranteed. It isn't like graduating with a conventional degree and then having a fairly regular, long and prosperous career. Even with film and television degrees, your career may not progress in a predictable linear timeline.

On the flip side, you may even decide you don't want to be in this business. The exhaustive, unpredictable long hours just don't work for you. Perhaps the chaos of it is too much and too stressful for you and your family. *This does not make you a failure.* Failure is *not* trying to accomplish goals you have set.

My sister Karen paid for my very first composite. It was a wonderful gift and she was so supportive. My brother Mike helped me with a car and a telephone when I couldn't afford it. He even drove across town to drive me to junior college so I could continue to study. Other family and friends gave me support just by watching my shows and sending encouraging words. My father-in-law loaned me money to train and shoot a beginning model's portfolio. Afterwards, I toured Europe and paid him back. After my husband passed away, I was fortunate to be able to rely on my family and supportive friends to baby-sit my children and dogs so I could work on all-night shoots or travel.

When you come home for the holidays, you come home to an excited group of friends and family who want to hear all about your so-called glamorous life. You get a part and everyone is thrilled, but then you are edited right out of it. They might not understand that being cut out does not mean you failed or weren't good enough. They might feel if you were edited out, you did "something wrong."

Why do people react the way they do? It is insufficient knowledge and understanding. Believe it or not, people believe what they see written in tabloids. You know the magazines and newspapers I am referring to. They base their perceptions about entertainers on what they read in a "Rag Mag" and may have difficulty grasping that what is in print may not be correct. I encourage you to join me in boycotting these horrible and hurtful publications.

The key to your own self-esteem should not rest in those around you. Instead, focus on the efforts you put into your work. When family and friends are not as supportive as you would like them to be, give them the benefit of the doubt. Their misunderstanding of your business probably isn't intended to be hurtful. They simply aren't informed.

Remember the oft misquoted saying: You can please some of the people all of the time and all of the people some of the time, but you can't please all of the people all of the time. The reality is you can't control anyone else's reactions. You can only strive to please yourself.

Following Up

A common theme for failure is *not* for lack of talent, it's *not* lack of beauty or education; it's because people simply *don't* follow-up. Follow-up is the single most difficult thing to do.

Follow-up is extremely difficult. I know this, because I have run several businesses, including my acting career. I find this important but tedious practice taxing on my brain and my emotions. The fear of the unknown makes it one of the hardest of the skills to master.

The little voice inside your head says: Will they remember me? Will they know who I am? Will they laugh at me over the phone? Will they not pick up because they now have Caller ID and know it's me calling? Will they refuse to open my envelope? Did I forget previously to send a letter or a thank you?

Acting is about showing up.

Following up is more than thank you notes and phone calls; it's a philosophy that must run through every fiber of your being. Following up is the height of professionalism, and if you can discipline yourself in this area consistently, you WILL stand out.

Want to know why? Simple: Because most people won't do it. As you wind your way through auditions and readings and cattle calls and callbacks, you will notice a lot of familiar faces, but just as many – sometimes twice as many – fresh, eager, *new* faces.

That's because even though many people think they can act; most don't want to put in the work. You'll find your auditions full of young, enthusiastic, pretty, perky people who simply don't have the motivation, skill, or desire to do that simplest of tasks – follow-through.

As a result, they're here today, gone tomorrow. It may seem like they get all the work; it may seem like you're in a bad patch or a slump, but trust me: Follow through on every audition, every reading, every callback, and you will get work.

Follow Up Habits

Here are easy ways to follow up that will prove invaluable as you expand your acting career:

1) **Just Checking In**: You simply must get over your fear of keeping in touch with your agent, manager, acting friends, and casting agents who have expressed interest in your talent. This is how work gets done; people know someone and recommend them for the job. If they don't know you; they can't recommend you. Check in with your agent as requested. Keep your team updated; not only will they know you are professional, they will know something just as valuable: You are available! You can check-in by phone, email, and your postcards.

2) **The Update**: Newsflash! Good news is a great excuse to follow up. Be it the completion of a particularly challenging acting class or that hot new indie film you just wrapped, share the news proudly. Just got a new part? Spent three days on the set of the latest blockbuster as an extra? *Tell someone! Tell everyone!* Add it to your résumé, and call your agent to tell him how it went (if he set it up) or give him the news (if you did). It's not bragging – it's your business.

3) **A Friendly Reminder**: Reminding is a lost art, but not if you begin practicing it right now, today. If you have a week-long part, remind your agent on Monday that you'll be on the set all week (this is called "booking out"). Not only will he appreciate the update, but you'll be on his mind all week. Got a friend who just won a major role? Remind her that you're available and rooting for her. (Not necessarily in that order, of course!) You get the picture.

> Feed your HUNGER to succeed with small successes on the creative road . . . and remember to enjoy these times, because you will look back at them as the HAPPIEST and MUST FULFILLING times of your Life . . . . Develop camaraderie with friends, and most importantly, WATCH THEIR BACKS, and find friends to help. WATCH YOUR BACK . . . because the creative person needs that camaraderie that nurtures the spirit and protects us from our own naivety.
>
> Jack Turnbull, Actorsite.com

CHAPTER 13

DEAR LAR

Dear Lar,

I need some audition advice. Acting is strange. It feels like it costs so much money to try to get noticed. It's like....if you're not rich, you can't make it in the film industry. Not that I am getting discouraged because acting is so much fun, it is my dream.

Honestly, it seems like a long lost highway to nowhere.
Sincerely,
Jeffery

Dear Jeffery,

The entertainment business is just like any other field. All businesses require startup capital (money), training, and trial and error.

Unfortunately most beginners and actually even some veterans do not realize this.

It is important to thoroughly look at the business to decide if the entertainment lifestyle is for you. It can be an exciting career, but the ups and downs do not stop, regardless of any success you may find. The training and skills required to work in film and the longer-than-average workweek can take their toll, especially when you don't perceive as immediate returns.

I did not have a dime to my name when I started. I had two pairs of jeans and two pairs of shoes for my entire sophomore year –I could not afford a blow dryer for my hair, I could not afford contacts and we didn't have a phone. I took a job at a modeling school in Dallas, where I agreed to work free for two years full-time to pay for my classes. I did not have a car and took two buses each way from work and transferred to another bus before getting to school. It's called "paying your dues" and that was only the beginning of paying mine!

I ended up being hired as a teacher and stayed there 6 years.

Also, I worked at night from 7-2am at a local restaurant and then went to high school at 8am.

A couple of years later I worked 8-5 as a receptionist and then drove to the school to teach classes from 6-9 pm, three days a week and all day Saturday. On Sundays, I worked 8 hours at a drugstore. I was 18 years old.

While trying to get my college degree- I finally got a car! I lived in my own apartment from the age of 17 (never moving home again and not supported by parents).

My first agent turned me down 8 times.

It is not money that is required to get going in this industry – it is drive, persistence, perseverance and an unwavering desire to do the work.

You can find ways – you can create ways and you will surprise yourself with what can be accomplished. Money is not the answer - the answer lies within and money is the excuse.

This is not a field for everyone and that is ok. You must always have a backup plan and always plan your budget - there will never be a steady check and when there is one, it will be soon gone.

Dear Lar,

Hi, my name is Ken and I am just getting started in acting. My friend has been acting for some time and he says I don't really need to have my headshot done every 6 months. Isn't it a waste of money?

Dear Ken,

Your friend is both correct and incorrect. Until digital photography took over, actors could use the same headshot for 2-4 years, especially if they were already known "name" actors. If someone had been in the biz for a while and all the casting directors knew him very well, an actor could get by without updating his headshot as often. But that has all changed. Today, submissions are electronic, and just to stand out from the massive numbers of actors trying be seen for a role, outstanding actors need outstanding materials. Even if your look hasn't changed drastically, fresh new headshots will always be more interesting than the same old one. So to gain a competitive edge in this business, update your advertising at least twice a year. Think of it like a store updating their front windows every season. You are the store.

Dear Lar,

I am a 13-year-old girl. My goal is to work in a Disney television show. A local agent says he has connections to the studio, and if I sign up for $1400 he will submit my headshot. He says I have the right look. My mom and I had a huge fight over it. She says he just wants the money. Please, Lar, tell me how to reach my goals.

Dear Future Star,

Mom wins this one, but you can still have a future as an actress. Legitimate agents do not charge any fees to submit their talent to any castings, period. Agents submit all of their talent anywhere they can find a role that may be a fit for you. I suggest you look for a real agent, and keep your wallet closed. You can even submit yourself to these studios simply by mailing your headshot and résumé until you get an agent. Go hug your Mom for saving you money and heartache, and get busy with a real agent.

Dear Lar,

      I am new to acting. By *new*, I mean I am 57 and I haven't acted once. I feel like I have always wanted to do this, and I know that I won't be happy until I give this my best shot. Please tell me what I need to do.

Dear 57 years young,

      New? No way! New career, yes, and that's okay. Take a look at all the actors on all the TV shows and movies. Someone has to play the older characters, because all the cosmetic fillers and facelifts. Hollywood may soon run out of aging actors. The real issue is where do you start? First, you will need to train. If you have not already done so, sign up for a basic acting class. Then you will need headshots, an agent, and you will need to pound the pavement like all the other successful actors. Do not let your age hold you back. Go for it!

Dear Lar,

      I looked in the phone book. There are exactly 3 agents in my area. Should I sign with one of them or should I go to the nearest city and try to find an agent there?

Dear Agent Searcher,

Just because there are only three where you live doesn't mean that they aren't any good. Have a meeting with each of them. There may be only three agents because there is not much work in your area. Plan on searching for your agent up to 300 miles from your home, which is not uncommon if you live outside Los Angeles or New York. It does mean a lot of driving, so ask yourself if you have the drive to succeed.

Dear Lar,

My favorite book is now being made into a movie. I'd love to be in that movie. I think I am perfect for the lead character. Is there any way I can ask my agent if he could get me a reading without looking like a total kook?

Dear Bookworm,

I suspect by the time you have read your favorite book, industry professionals have, too, and a script is probably already in the works. Lead roles are generally reserved for actors with a great deal of experience. Ask your agent to do some research on the project. You can also write the author and see if the movie rights have been purchased. If not, purchase the rights and make the movie yourself.

Dear Lar,

I am a 30-year-old actress. I have a great deal of experience, having done numerous plays both on and off

Broadway. I am used to auditioning at least once a week. However, now that I made the switch to television and moved to Los Angeles, I find that my agent seldom sends me on auditions. I go to cattle calls on my own, so I know the auditions are happening. Is my agent doing her job or just stringing me along?

Dear Broadway Star,

Are your materials up to date? Do you have a marketing plan including drops and postcards? Does your agent know you are alive? What is your callback ratio on auditions? You have a great deal to consider, so start by talking to your agent. Are they passionate about you? If not, start the search for a better one. Second, learn and study the different auditioning techniques between New York and Los Angeles.

Dear Lar,

Naked! My first big break and they want me to get naked. The idea of Performing nude makes me very uncomfortable. What do I do? I don't want to get blacklisted.

Dear Naked,

Just say no. If it really is a "big break" they can and will have a body double, and everyone will still think it is you. Your only chance of being blacklisted is if your future is in pornography.

Dear Lar,

I'll make this short and sweet. I live in Shreveport. Should I move to Los Angeles or New York?

Dear Out of Big City,

Both yes and no. Ask yourself what you have to offer each city. Extensive training? Strong résumé? You may want to build these areas before moving and competing in a larger market. Remember, you aren't going to marry the city. You can always move home in a few months if you don't like it.

Dear Lar,

I have two small children. How can I build an acting career close to home? I have a supportive family, but until my kids are older, moving is out of the question.

Dear Mom,

Honestly, unless you already live in Los Angeles, New York or a large city, you have few choices. I was already successful when I had my children and it was and is still difficult. The best advice is to keep training and to produce or direct something; do whatever project comes your way. Look into voiceover work, too, which can be done remotely.

Dear Lar,

I was an extra last week, and I heard some of the actors talking about a new actress making a big mistake. They were laughing about it, and said she would probably not be asked to be in a film again. How can I make sure this doesn't happen to me?

Dear Extra,

You can't. Gossip spreads faster than fire in Hollywood. I once said I had a headache at 7 AM in the make-up chair, and that night the producer called me to see if I had the brain tumor results. Be on time, know your material, do not gossip, keep your chin up, and be loyal to your fellow actors.

Dear Lar,

My 8-year-old daughter is star-struck. My husband and I have decided we want to support her. She is a very gregarious child, and she has a good singing voice. It is possible she has what it takes. I am concerned with how destructive the business seems to be to the lives of some child actors. How can I protect her while still encouraging her to live her dreams?

Dear Concerned Parent,

It's not really that the business is destructive. Individuals can choose to lead destructive lives. The sheer fact that you are so concerned is a good foundation for your child's security. *You* are in charge of her career at this age, her photo shoots, her auditions, the roles she accepts, and the people she works with and is coached by.

We learn by following healthy role models, and as long as you continue to monitor her environment, she should be fine.

Dear Lar,

Help! I think I need an agent. I was at a club the other night, and this director came up to me and gave me his business card. He wants me to drop by his office for a photo shoot. What should I do first? I've never acted before.

Dear Right Place/Right Time,

First of all, big red flag! Directors are NOT photographers, so you are right to be concerned. Use his business card to research him. If he is really who he says he is, congratulations. You may have just gotten your big break. If this is a scam, you've saved yourself a lot of time, money, and heartache. Unless a professional agent has set up the interview or audition, never go to an office alone. For your safety, use the buddy system.

Dear Lar,

My daughter is 14 years old and I just saw her headshots. She looks way too grown up! Is this supposed to happen? I don't want her to be objectified. Then I went to her acting class and she was playing a hooker. I was shocked to see her saying words we don't allow in our home. I feel like they have her growing up too fast. I just want to yell "STOP" and tell her she can't do this any more. What can I do to protect my daughter while she is going through her teen years?

Dear Protective Parent,

Photo shoots vary for actors and models. Models will generally have more make-up, look more mature, and be fashion-oriented. There is no reason a teen should look like a mature adult in a headshot, the goal of which is to look natural and not made up. From what you were saying, you have good reason to be concerned about the headshots. For future photo shoots, stay with your minor child the entire time.

As for the acting class, playing dramatic roles is acceptable and to be expected. Playing characters unlike yourself is part of the job. It may have made you uncomfortable, because you had not seen your daughter perform before in a professional setting. Many teenage roles will explore the lives of angst-ridden, drug addicted, run-away, and rebellious characters. It's pretty common; I have also had to play similar roles, as have most successful actors. You may find comfort in knowing that the more difficult roles are extremely rewarding and involve a great deal of research, soul-searching, and compassion. Your daughter will learn a lot about herself in the process of exploring a character who is unlike her.

CAREER...

As we end our time together, that is my wish for you: A CAREER in this wonderful, eclectic, challenging, rewarding, intimidating, magical, marvelous field. Not just a job, not just a role, not just an audition, but a *career*.

When we started this journey, a career may have been the furthest thing from your mind. Perhaps you just wanted to know how to get a headshot, an agent, or become a star.

Hopefully by now I've shown you that acting and modeling can be so much more. Look at the list of jobs we read together in Part One again. Maybe one of those appealed to you even more than acting.

Think about the directors, wardrobe, makeup, and casting people you've met along this exhilarating, mysterious journey. Maybe one of their jobs appealed to you. Then again, maybe the acting bug is in your system for good. Bravo! You've taken the first step in what is hopefully a perfectly paved road ahead. Here's to you, and here's to your career.

May it be as long as you you'd hoped for . . .

And longer than you'd dared to dream . . .

Glossary of Terms

8 X 10 – Also called a headshot. It refers to the standard size of the photo commercial print models and actors are required to provide to agents and casting directors.

Account Executive – An employee of the advertising agency who works for a particular brand, like Sony. The accounts are referred to by the name of the client or the product ("the Sony account," "the Revlon® account"). Account executives may be present at photo shoots and castings to ensure that the model and the photographer are successfully carrying out the wishes of the client. See **Advertising Agency**.

Action – instructs actors to begin the scene.

Actor – A person who performs material. This career requires life long training. You must learn camera angles, how to prepare a character, and many other skills. Usually if you are making a career out of acting, you will join the Screen Actors Guild, which is a union. You may not join just because you want to. You must have a work history to be eligible for membership.

Advertising Agency – the company that specializes in creating ads for big brands. Almost all of the ads you see on TV or in magazines are created by an advertising agency. Modeling agencies send headshots and talent they think would be a good match for a particular product or ad campaign to the ad agency. The ad agency casts the models. They hire a photographer, who will secure the location, hire a stylist and make-up artist, and coordinate the shoot. On a job like this, the model is working for the photographer, the modeling agency, the advertising agency, and the original client, all of whom may show up at the photo shoot to see how the product looks on or with the model.

AFTRA (US) / ACTRA (CANADA) – The American Federation of Television and Radio Artists (AFTRA) / Alliance of Canadian Cinema Television and Radio Artist (ACTRA). These are the unions that actors must belong to in order to get hired for a union television job (SAG is another one).

Agency – A company that represents models, actors and talent. The agency is responsible for representing and promoting its roster of talent and booking auditions and jobs for them. Agencies handle contracts and payments.

Agent – The person who represents you. You may have a specific agent who handles you or several agents at your agency may share workload. A modeling agent is the same thing as a booking agent. "Agent" is sometimes used incorrectly and interchangeably with the term "manager." They are actually *very different positions* and should not be confused with one another.

APD – Academy Players Directory. This is both a book and an online listing of industry professionals (agents, managers, casting directors and actors). It can be found at www.playersdirectory.com.

Audition – A tryout for a film, TV or stage part. When a model auditions for a modeling booking, it's often called a go-see.

B&W – Black and white, as in a black & white photograph (the only other alternative is color). Used to be photos used as an actor's headshot were almost always in black and white. Today color has become the norm.

Backdrop – The "scene or paper drop" behind the model during a photo shoot. In a studio, this is usually seamless paper or a faux location scene. Do not step onto the backdrop in your shoes! Check with the photographer first.

Background/Atmosphere/Extra – Non-principal actors in a photograph, a TV show, a movie or a play. (As in, "I worked two days as background on a new pilot.")

Barefaced – See "clean-clean."

Beauty Shot – A close-up shot of part or all of the face (lips, eyes, etc.). This kind of photo is usually used in a cosmetics print ad or in a magazine editorial about skincare products, make-up products, etc.

Bite Sized Media – See "snack sized media."

Blogs/Weblogs – An online daily diary. These can be used to keep your readers up to date on your career. Actors should never use them for personal ramblings or political diatribes – stick to news about yourself.

Book – To reserve a model's time by hiring her for a job; also the book or portfolio a model carries to go-sees, jobs, etc.

Booking – A job. When you get a job, you say you "booked" a job.

Bookout – When you inform your agent you're not available for a job, for either professional or personal reasons, and the agent cannot book you during that time. You've "booked out" for that time. As a professional, you need to be responsible for your own time. Don't expect your agent or your clients to remember that you're going home for your Grandma's birthday next week or that you booked a job through your other agency that day. To help prevent cancellations and angry clients, you should keep every booking agent you work with aware of your schedule. This is a task you should do regularly. You can do this several ways, not just by calling. Use email, fax, answering machine, voicemail.

Buyout – An agreement by an agent and a model that allows their client to use the TV commercial or photograph that the model appeared in wherever and however they want, for a specific time period, and for a fee.

Call Back – A second, third, fourth (and so on) audition for a job. When a client has seen everyone for a particular job, they will then call the people they feel best fit the role come back and audition again. There can be more than one call back. Always wear the same clothing and take more headshots and résumés regardless of the number of call backs you are asked to attend.

Call Sheet – The sheet that goes out to all people involved in a photo shoot or filming that gives the details of the shoot. Important information on the call sheet includes your call time, the location of the shoot, and how you should appear upon arrival. Clients may want the models to arrive already in full make-up and hair or they may want the models to show up barefaced (see clean-clean). If you don't know this information by the day before the shoot, call your agent and find out. Don't wait until so late in the evening that you can't reach someone. Don't set yourself up to be "ready to blame" someone. Not following directions causes a lot of expensive, wasted time in the studio and may stop you from getting hired by that client again.

Call Time – this is the exact time you need to show up for work. Consider your personal call time 15 minutes before your official call time!

Casting Call – An announcement put out to actors or models for a specific role or job. Casting and modeling agencies usually host the casting calls, which may also occur at production offices, studios, hotel suites, etc. A closed casting call is one in which the talent has been handpicked and invited to appear. An open casting call (AKA "Cattle Call") is usually advertised in the trades (papers) and is open to anyone.

Character Model/Character Actor – Character models and actors are hired to play the nerd, the fat guy, the librarian, or the little old lady from Pasadena. These talented folks have many different characters they can play. Character actors and models rarely become household names, but this can be an extremely lucrative area.

Cinematographer – also called the director of photography. This person works with the director. This crew person lights the scene, chooses the appropriate lenses and recording medium for the shoot, and is responsible for how the film or television show looks on film or video.

Clean-Clean – A specification on a call-sheet that means clean hair, clean face, clean, simple groomed nails, etc. You should show up for the photo shoot with no make-up on and freshly washed hair and short, clean, clear nails. Lose the fake plastic tip extensions; these are old and out-of-date. The opposite of this is "hair and make-up ready," which is self-explanatory.

Client – The one who pays your salary. A model can have several types of clients. Modeling agencies have clients, too. These can be anyone who wants to hire a model for a job, like a fashion magazine, a designer, an ad agency, and
1) The person or company who hires you for the job. These kinds of clients include: fashion magazines, fashion designers, clothing catalogues or advertising agencies; and
2) The model. When modeling agents refer to their "clients," they are usually referring to the models they represent, but it could also mean the magazines and advertisers that hire their models. Whenever you're on a shoot, treat the clients with respect. They are the ones paying you and they will not hesitate to fire you if you behave unprofessionally or waste their very valuable time.

3) The product manufacturers who hire the ad agencies to produce the ad. A representative from the client company usually shows up at photo shoots to ensure that the photos are making their products look good.

Close-Up – The actor's face fills the shot.

Comp Card/Zed Card/Postcard – A reproduced photo layout that usually has various pictures of you in different looks and different types of jobs.

Coogan's Law – Protects minors' earnings and establishes trust accounts in an effort to prohibit mismanagement of child entertainers' wages.

Craft Services – provides food and snacks for principal cast and crew.

Cut – instructs actors to stop dialog and movement.

Demo – 1-3 minutes of edited tape of film/TV work you have done; highlight only the best.

Documentary – Is a film or television style using the recording of actual events. Documentaries are based on a true story, event or belief.

Editing – is the process of cutting film or video footage and reassembling the pieces into an artistic and/or informative story line.

Editor – The person who takes the "raw footage" and assembles the various shots into film where all the elements; such as vocal sound, visual images, and music come together as a finished product.

Establishing Shot – The initial shot that establishes where the characters are located in a particular scene. This shot shows the whole area where the scene takes place.

Fill Lighting – These are the lights that fill in the scene and removing or add shadows for the shot.

Genre – This is a term used to describe a type of film based on the way a story is told using narrative, types of characters, plot lines and even settings common to certain types of movies, books and television shows. Romance, Comedy, and Action Adventure are examples of genres.

Go-See – An appointment that you have to "go-see" someone and show (him or her) your portfolio.

Headshot – Reproduced headshots of what you really look like with your agency name and number so clients can call you. This picture should be updated at least twice a year.

Internet Movie Data Base (IMDB) – The recognized industry website for information on people, events and projects. Fans can track the careers of their favorite actors, directors and other film professionals.

IActor.com – The Screen Actor's Guild (SAG) online casting site for union members only.

Key Light – The key light is the main light that lights the faces of the actors.

Manager – Managers are for actors that work a lot. Managers can take up to an additional 15% of your pay in addition to your agent.

Medium Shot – An actor is shown from the waist up.

Mobisode – A short (three minute or less) TV episode especially made for viewing on mobile phones.

Model – A person that is used either in photography, films or "live" to sell or demonstrate products.

Montage – A group of visual images and or shots edited together to build dramatic tension and often used to condense time and the transpiring events on the screen.

Podcast – Downloadable media such as entertainment, news casts, instructional programming and so on for use on portable devices.

Point Of View – Also known as P.O.V. It is the character's view of the action in the scene.

Portfolio – A collection of photos and samples of work you have actually done. Must be continually updated and is usually in an 8X10 size.

Producer – The person who oversees the entire project including the making of the film and financing of the film.

Production Designer – The person responsible for the room settings and exteriors that help give the film its look in regards to time, place and feel.

Proof Sheet /Contact Sheets – An 8X10 sheet that shows all of the pictures you shot on a roll of film (you pick the best ones from the sheet and you do not need a lot of pictures from the same sheet). Now mostly done on digital.

Résumé – Marketing tool designed with two major goals in mind, to get you a job or audition. It presents your skills, experience and accomplishments. It must be cut to 8x10 and attached to your headshot.

Script Revisions – Line changes that affect the story

Snack Size Media – The theory that people will not watch full-length movies on their mobile devices but will watch short length programs.

Social Networks – Communities where people can meet online, exchange digital files and information, and launch new programming through viral marketing.

Take – Is a shot of a scene in a film. The editor and director choose from the original takes to assemble the film.

Tear Sheets – These are when you "tear out" from newspapers or magazines the work you have done and keep them in your portfolio. This term is referring to a portfolio of completed jobs.

The Book – The book agencies distribute to all of their clients to promote their models. The book contains the comp card for each model represented by the agency. Models may be required to pay a fee to have their comp card printed in the book. The equivalent to a head book for actors is the Academy Players Directory for union talent and the web pages for individual agencies. If there is a cost, it should be very minimal and not a monthly fee.

Trades – Legitimate newspapers and magazines (like *Variety*) that report on the business of the acting industry.

Viral Marketing - A form of generating exposure via word of mouth buzz through podcasts, webcasts, blogs, social networks, and e-mail. They are usually scripted, and often perceived to be amateur, but a well-produced one can be seen by millions overnight. Based on a concept that people will spread the information quickly if it is entertaining or informative.

Voiceover (VO) – voice over /off camera

Voiceover Demo – 1-3 minutes of recorded voice work.

Voucher – A form that you will fill out to show the times you were there and any related expenses. This is usually obtained from your agent.

Webcast- Similar to watching a television show, multiple users can view the same content at the same time.

Webisode – Concise, scripted entertainment shot specifically for Internet viewing

Wrap - filming is over for the day

Test your set vocabulary using this fun puzzle. Answers on page 176.

www.CrosswordWeaver.com

ACROSS

1 It's a _____ means filming is over for the day

5 This is the term that instructs actors to stop dialog and movement

7 _____ boy are crew members who assist the electrical department

8 _____ __ _____ is the term that indicates it's okay to move and speak quietly; it's similar to a double bell

9 This is a term used to begin filming

11 This is the camera operator's indication to the director that the scene can begin

12 _____ bell is warning everyone that filming is beginning

13 These are the teamsters that move heavy equipment to various locations

DOWN

2 This is the term that instructs actors to begin the scene

3 _____ __ _____ is the term that indicates filming is about to begin and those on set should be still and quiet

4 _____ bell means you may move around and talk quietly

6 _____ or solid red light means do not enter or exit the sound stage

7 This is the same thing as a bell

9 _____ revisions are line changes you must memorize

10 _____ service is the food and snack table

Internet Resources

For additional online information, the following sites are legitimate actors and industry resources sites:

www.AcademyPlayersDirectory.com
www.nowcasting.com
www.breakdownservices.com

www.actorsaccess.com
www.iactor.com
www.aftra.org (American Federation of Television and Radio Artists)

www.SAG.org (Screen Actors Guild)
www.SAGindy.org
www.wga.org (Writers Guild of America)

www.geniebeauty.com (Genie Beauty Products)

www.GetStartedNotScammed.com
www.LarParkLincoln.com
www.TalentStart.net

Acknowledgements

It has been said "It takes a village" and it does. No career is created by one person, and I have many people to thank for their guidance, support, friendship and professional expertise. So here is my heartfelt *thank you* to my village.

My sister Karen for her unwavering belief in my ability. My brothers Mike and Pat. My agents at The William Morris Agency and my managers. My agent Suzanne Horne. The expert coaches: Margie Haber, Tony Barr, Marilynn Henry, and Sam Christensen for awesome coaching and career guidance. The casting directors that went to bat many times for a then unknown young actress and the directors and producers that cast me.

Castmates that taught me the ropes. Makeup artists that covered every flaw, wardrobe designers that helped me hide two pregnancies, and a slew of talented crew members that created the magic off screen so I could shine on screen.

A special 5th grade teacher, Mr. D, who taught me how to memorize pages and pages of dialogue. The QVC Network for giving me a voice and a fun show to work on.

My parents, who instilled in me a work ethic that allowed me to pursue this incredible journey. Mary Ann and Joe, dear friends and partners. Casey, Jimmy, Ayn, Nancy.

To the many people that have crossed my path and taught and guided me, I am forever grateful.

A Big Texas Thank You to Our Agents
Campell Agency, www.TheCampbellAgency.com
Clutts Agency, www.TheCluttsAgency.com
Core Talent, www.CoreTalent.biz
Horne Agency, www.HorneAgency.com
Ivette Stone, www.IvetteStoneAgency.com
Kim Dawson, www.KimDawsonAgency.com
Linda McAlister, www.LindaMcAlisterTalent.com
Mary Collins, www.MaryCollins.com
Tomas Agency, www.TomasAgencyTalent.com

Thank You

This book could not have been possible without the help of many talented people.

The families that bravely came forward to share their experiences to help others not get scammed.

Brad Barton for interior design, continual rewrites, last minute additions, and keeping the schedule on track. Alissa Barton for braving a thunderstorm for an emergency proofing session.

Special encouragement from Suzi Zimmerman, Libby Mitchell, Tamara Dickey, Toni Cyan Brock, Landy Johnson, Judith Moose, Laura Fox, Denise Kovac, Bernadette Volker, My QVC family and coworkers, Nancy Johnson, Kathy Tyner, David Baertsch, and all of my awesome students that will be or already are stars!

Photographers

Brad Barton	Debbie Patton
Ashley Case	Mark Roddenberry
Mary Ann Halpin	Kerby Shultz
Cody Harris Studios	Kelly Squires Taylor
Heather Nix	Carsten von Hedemann

"An Expert Says" Contributors

Sam Christensen: www.SamChristensen.com
Bonnie Gillespie: www.CricketFeet.com
Steven Mays: www.namiss.com
Brad Barton: www.txheadshots.com
Bob Fraser: www.YouMustAct.com
Cynthia Brian: www.CynthiaBrian.com
Margie Haber: www.MargieHaber.com
Jill Jaress: www.JillJaress.com
Mary Ann Halpin: www.MaryAnnHalpin.com
Tony Barr/Eric Stephen Klein: www.FilmActorsWorkshop.com
Jack Turnbull: www.Actorsite.com

About the Author
Lar Park Lincoln

2008 is quickly surpassing even the busiest of her 30 years in the entertainment field for Lar Park Lincoln! Already an Actress, QVC celebrity guest host, career coach, and speaker; this year, Lar has added author, director, and producer to her ever-growing list of achievements.

Her five-year role on *Knots Landing* offered her the opportunity to work with such luminaries as Michelle Lee, William Devane, Kathleen Quinlan, Mario Van Peebles, Rod Taylor, Michael Landon, and Angela Lansbury. She has been a featured guest on "Oprah" and "Entertainment Tonight", plus numerous local and syndicated talk and radio shows.

Lar decided to return to her native state of Texas to raise her children. Since that move, she rapidly became Texas' most elite career coach for actors, models, and pageantry.

With a script from her then 17-year-old film-student nephew Austin, Lar executive produced "Static," a film about teen heroin abuse. "We used all teens. The movie was teen-written, teen-edited and teen-developed. It kept its pulse firmly rooted in the reality of the teen drug culture."

She co-directed and competed in the Dallas twenty-four hour film race with a serious piece about racial discrimination, "Black and White."

Under her coaching wing, her daughter Piper, took the title of Miss Texas Jr. Teen and worked with Scottish Rite hospital helping children. Lar's son, Trevor, is on the road to becoming an Eagle Scout and is a guitar-strumming, trombone-playing All-American boy!!

Lar recently completed post production on her new role in Lifetime's *Inspector Mom,* a new series shot in her home state of Texas!

Two darling children, two standard poodles, one worthless but adorable guinea pig, and many unpacked suitcases make for laughs, sitcom situations, and one dynamic spokesperson!

Daisy Lincoln

Baby Lincoln

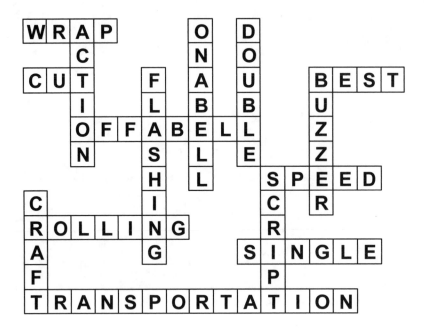

The *LarStar* Award

The *LarStar* Award is a program designed to guide deserving young talents pursuing a career in front of an audience or camera by building self confidence and developing terrific marketing materials. To nominate yourself or someone you know, please go to www.TalentStart.net and click on the *LarStar* Award application. Applications are accepted January 1 through May 15 each year and the winner is announced on June 15 of the same year.

The winner receives a complete career package, including on camera coaching, headshots, wardrobe consultation, acting lessons, and much more. Judging is based on answers to essay questions and financial need.

For More Information

To book Ms. Park Lincoln for coaching, speaking engagements, and appearances, go to www.LarParkLincoln.com.

To contact any of the actors or models appearing in this book, please email the studio at contactlar@larparklincoln.com

Lar coaching Ashlan on the set of *Inspector Mom*

© Brad Barton